# Marina Shkrobova-Vernalis

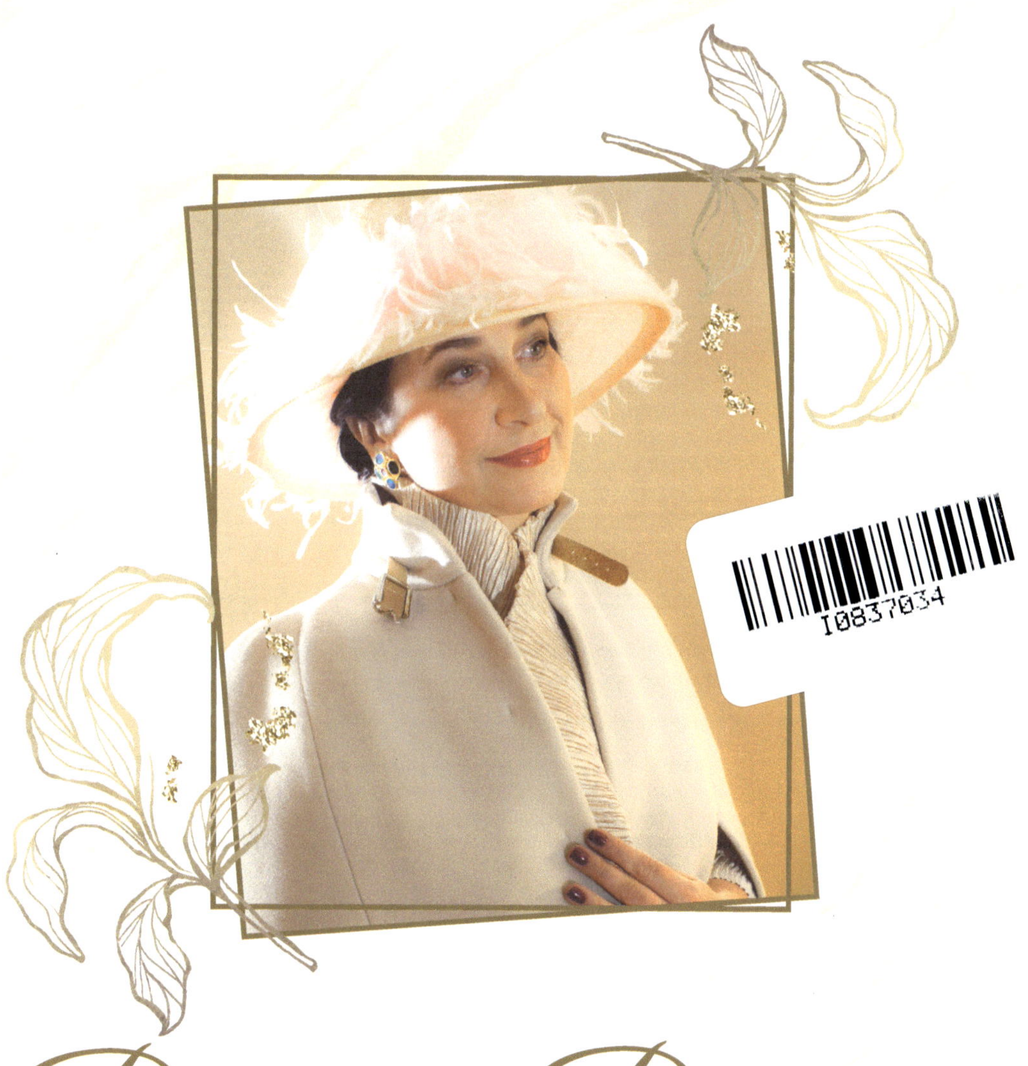


# Poetry in Paintings

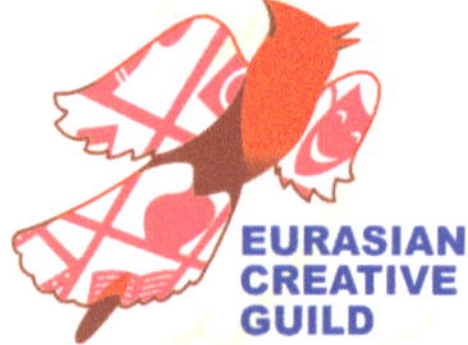


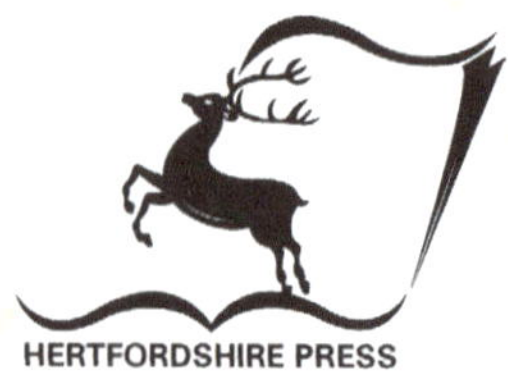


Published by Hertfordshire Press Ltd © 2023
e-mail: publisher@hertfordshirepress.com
www.hertfordshirepress.com

# Poetry in Paintings

Marina Shkrobova-Vernalis

*The book reveals the multifaceted soul of the poet and artist Marina Shkrobovoy-Vernalis. The author is a philosopher who looks at the magic sphere of life through the prism of poetry and painting! Hence the interest in various subjects in painting: landscapes, still lifes, flower compositions and portraits, written exclusively with love from the heart.*

*The deep interrelationship of meanings and images is interesting: in the image, the wisdom of loneliness lives in an autumn alley, the soul-insomnia is embodied in the image of a young goddess, and in portraits, even the color of the background hides a mystery!*

*Spiritual height lives here! And the author addresses everyone as a soul that he knows and feels for a long time as a relative!*

*This is a unique conversation with subjects who are ready to recognize themselves and reflect the beauty of their thoughts to the world!*

---



*British Library Catalogue in Publication Data*
*A catalogue record for this book is available from the British Library*
*Library of Congress in Publication Data*
*A catalogue record for this book has been requested*

**ISBN: 978-1-913356-70-5**

Marina Shkrobova-Vernalis

# Poetry in Paintings

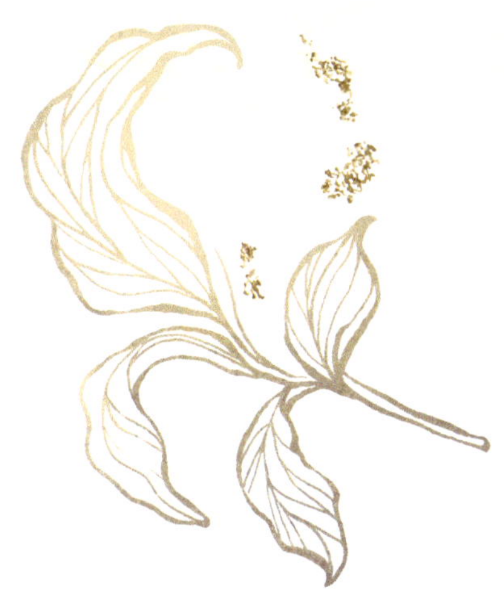

Лондон 2023

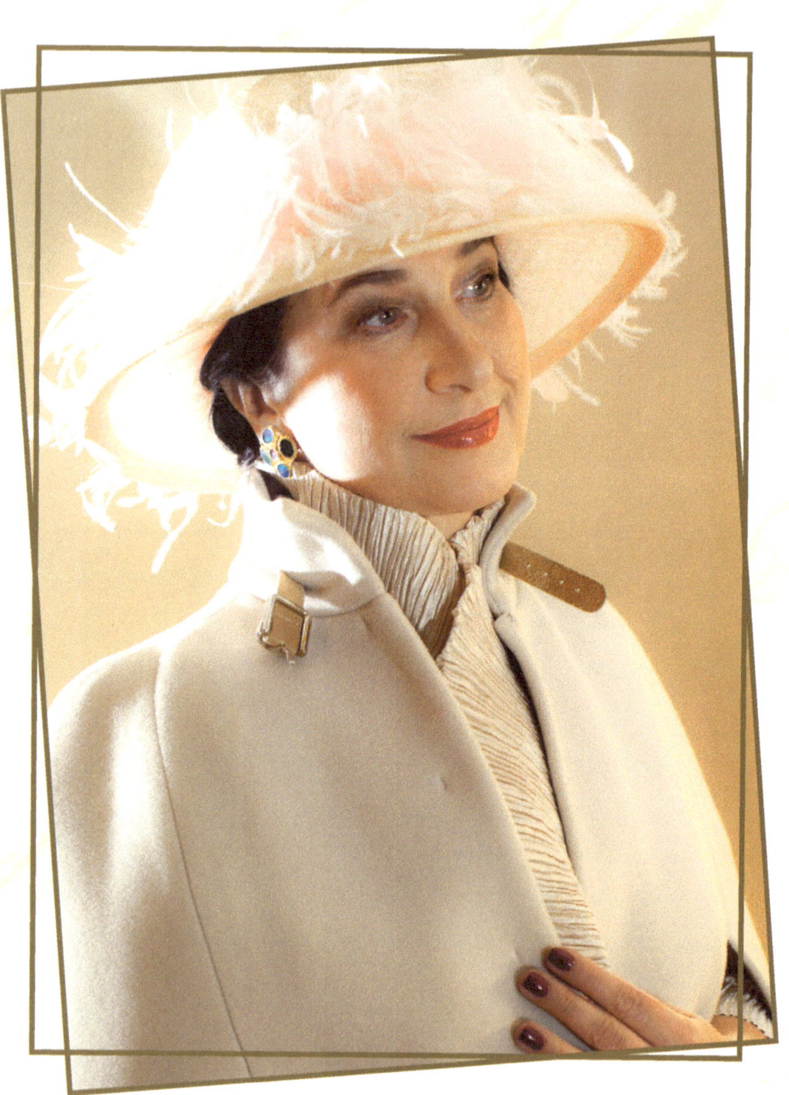

## I WANT TO TALK WITH YOU!

I want to talk with you!
Forgive me for speaking so openly,
For even when I try to be silent too,
Words all the same come out of me.

And the gathering of lands,
Of thoughts as yet unsaid!
You are now in my hands!
And again I begin to paint,

To draw each day as it comes,
Searching for the shades for all events!
You are my someone to talk to!
I trust my instincts...

I speak to you everywhere.
The shackles of the soul are unthinkable!
I thank you for everything!
We've known each for so long...

# About Author

For me painting is a meditation, an immersion into myself, or a return to my original self. And at the same time it is a dialogue with people, with the world, my semantic emphases!

In front of a blank canvas (just like in front of a blank page) I always feel awe and a passion to create. I create avidly, enjoying the process of creating a painting. Each stage is a wonder: at the mystery of touching the canvas, at the process of mixing the colours… even the smell of it!

I paint without noticing the time or feeling tired! Tiredness comes later, but there is always the unconcealed joy of 'making it happen' as a job well done (this is the pleasure my soul craves!).

My biggest surprise in painting has been coming to understand that the entire image is a combination of light and shadow! They are inseparable: if you want to show light, give me shadow! The depth of line and object appears when the light is supplemented or emphasised by the shadow. From the simplicity of the solution found! From the divine guidance of my hand!

I'm interested in different subjects and want to do everything! I love landscapes, especially sea and water scenes. I'm particularly fascinated by reflections - they have lots of imagination and magic in them! I love flower arrangements - it's like putting together an ikebana, feeling the floral ethereality and awe, and at the same time, the unique character of each flower.

I didn't think I would ever be brave enough to paint portraits! But now it's my favourite type of painting. Seeing an image emerge from the strokes, recognising it on the canvas and seeing what my soul, my love for that person is painting. That's how, out of love, an entire gallery of Silver Age poets was born. They are painted in a monochrome palette, but each poet demanded a different shade of paint, a different background. Boris Pasternak's romanticism and lyricism of nature. Alekandr Blok is classically depicted and serious in his gaze and appearance. The young and reverent Sergei Esenin, exquisitely ironic, with a flavour of aesthetics. The harmonious, spiritualized Anna Akhmatova, and the immeasurable and mysterious Marina Tsvetaeva. By the way, her background in the painting turned out to be different from all of the rest. By instinct! The artist's brush picked up this goldish hue to show that even in this series she still stands out for her poetic uniqueness. Nikolai Gumilev looks bold, his eyes seemingly with a mist in them. Such a «conquistador in an iron shell»! But here he turned out quite unprotected.... I remember the review sent to me by the actress Elena Denisova-Radzinskaya, who saw the first exhibition of portraits during 'Book Night' at the A. P. Bogolyubov State Art Library: «The portraits are fascinating! They are classical and modern at the same time! Thank you very much! I liked everything! Just very much!»

From my very first steps (strokes!) I fell in love with the palette knife. It helps me find my style in painting and be bold! In this way more than 80 paintings were born in eight years, and in spring 2017 my first personal exhibition of paintings opened in Moscow at the A.P. Bogolyubov State Art Library. In the spring of 2022 there was a second exhibition at the N.A. Dobrolyubov State Library.

My courage to put paint to canvas started with a painting class with the talented artist Alina Olenina. She knows not only how to draw, but how to discover everyone's unique gift! I will always be grateful to her. Truly, the Creator is infinitely generous to each of us; you just need to believe in your talent! Now I have two strong wings in my life: Poetry and Painting. And the world in illumination and thirst for creativity is amazing and beautiful!

With love,

*Marina Shkrobova-Vernalis*

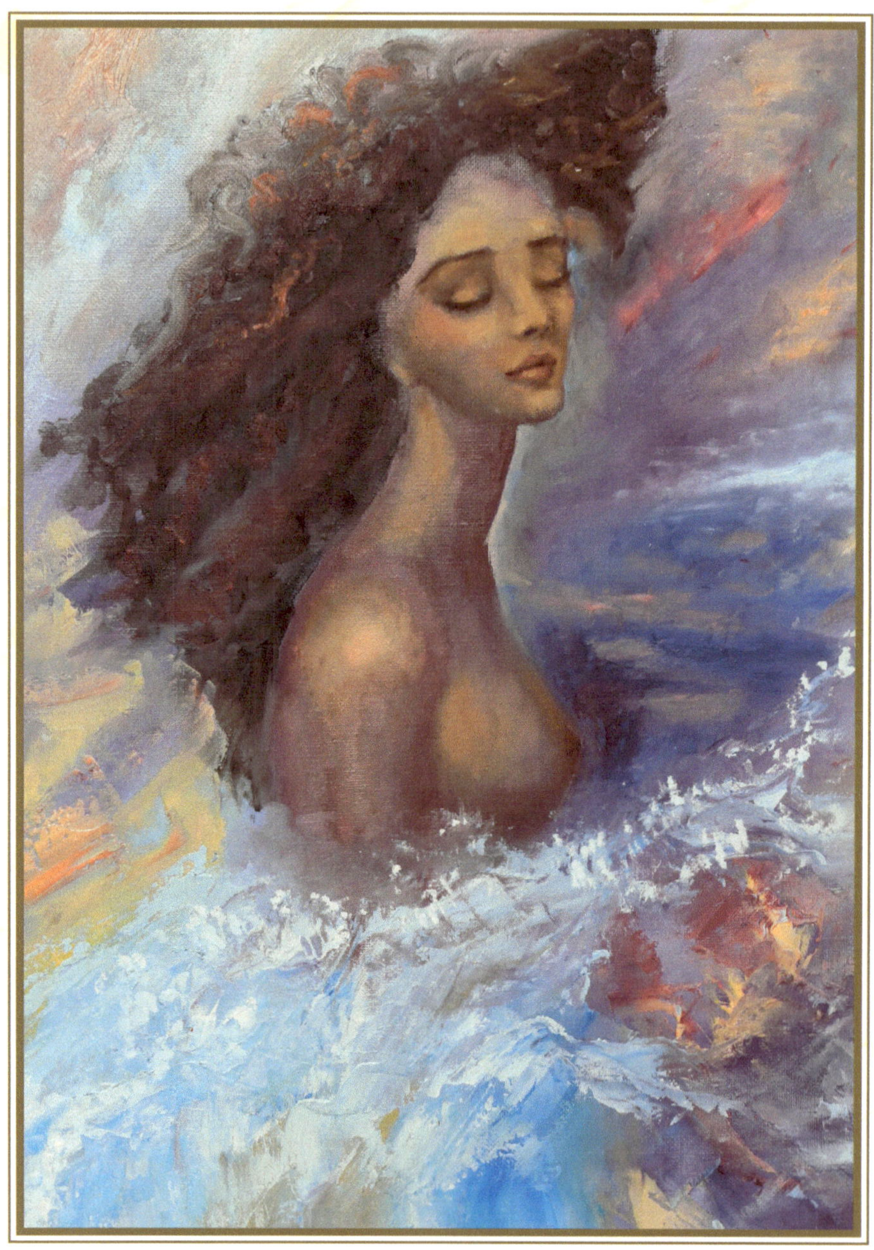

"Soul" Oil, Canvas. 60x90

## THE SOUL

The soul is an insomniac,
The soul is sleepless.
On the road, the wanderer,
In the Temple, the bell-ringer!

The soul is a sinner,
The soul is a slave.
The gatekeeper to some,
To others a pretender!

Cover yourself, you fool!
Don't tell everything!
Don't show your depths
Don't show them to everyone!

The soul is a wanderer,
The soul is a wanderer.
Some will repent
Who worships whom?

The soul is a renegade,
The soul is the intercessor.
In suffering, a prisoner,
The wandering companion

Silence, beauty!
Silence, bellringer!
Not every soul
Will open in response…

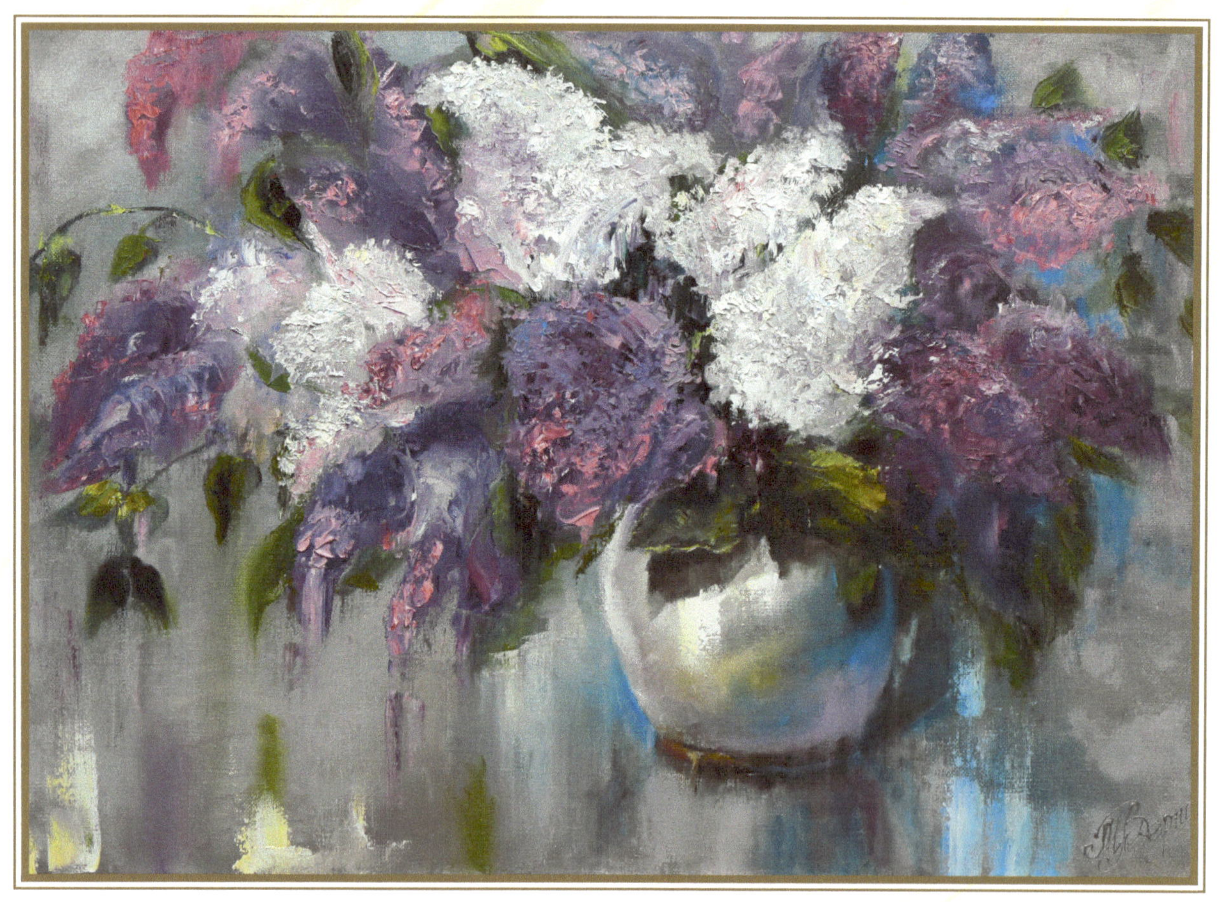

"Lilac" Oil, Canvas. 50x90 (Sold)

## LILAC MOOD

The lilac beds of spring!
Through the lush line of curly-headed bushes
We walk in the arms of those who are in love.
Lilacs always bloom for those in love!

In a wave of green avenues
That freshness of awakening!
And in a moment the sunset is alight
And the birds of the dawn sing more loudly!

Lilacs gather at your feet again!
With its heady, swirling, lilac foxtrot.
Touching the blush of tender cheeks
And trusting the kisser's vow

To cherish love! And the sentinels of love
With its light haze.
And that plume of lilac spring
Until new blossoms!

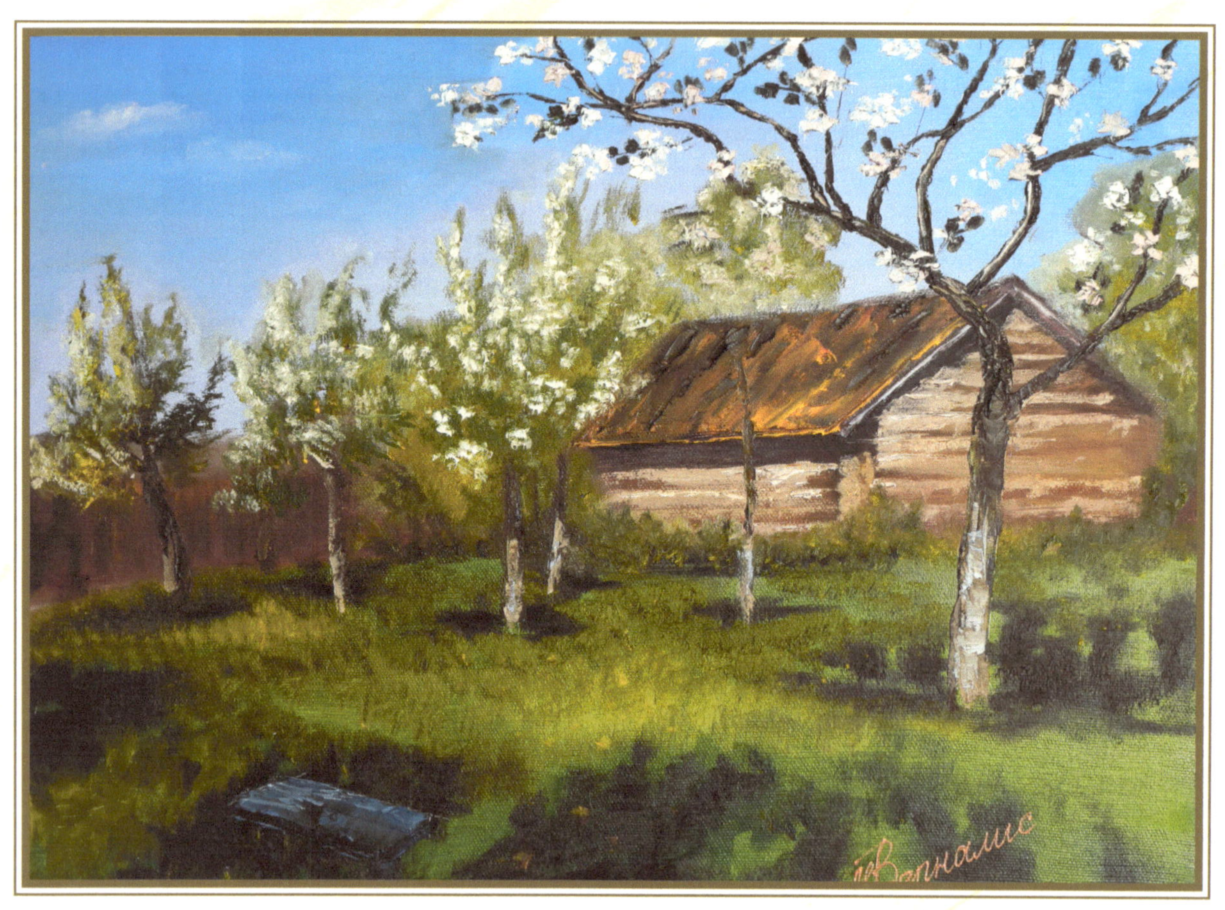


"Cherry Garden" Oil, Canvas. 60x90

The curtain on the window is fading,
Like wrinkles or cracks in paint
And the wine on the old terrace
Is already mature!

Languishing in the midday heat,
The house is hushed in the shade of ripening cherries,
Not even words spoken loudly can be heard
Amidst the apple trees.

Grace! The diligence and toil
Have brought a new harvest.
All that life has nurtured is reaped:
That's the result of our great game!

The crimson bush has blessed the garden,
And the garden's aster trees
As if it didn't know that time is moving on
And cannot go back!

So am I! I am flying at full gallop!
And the native landscape wrinkles with paint,
And calls me to the road, the uncontrollable road
Of the mind and the heart!

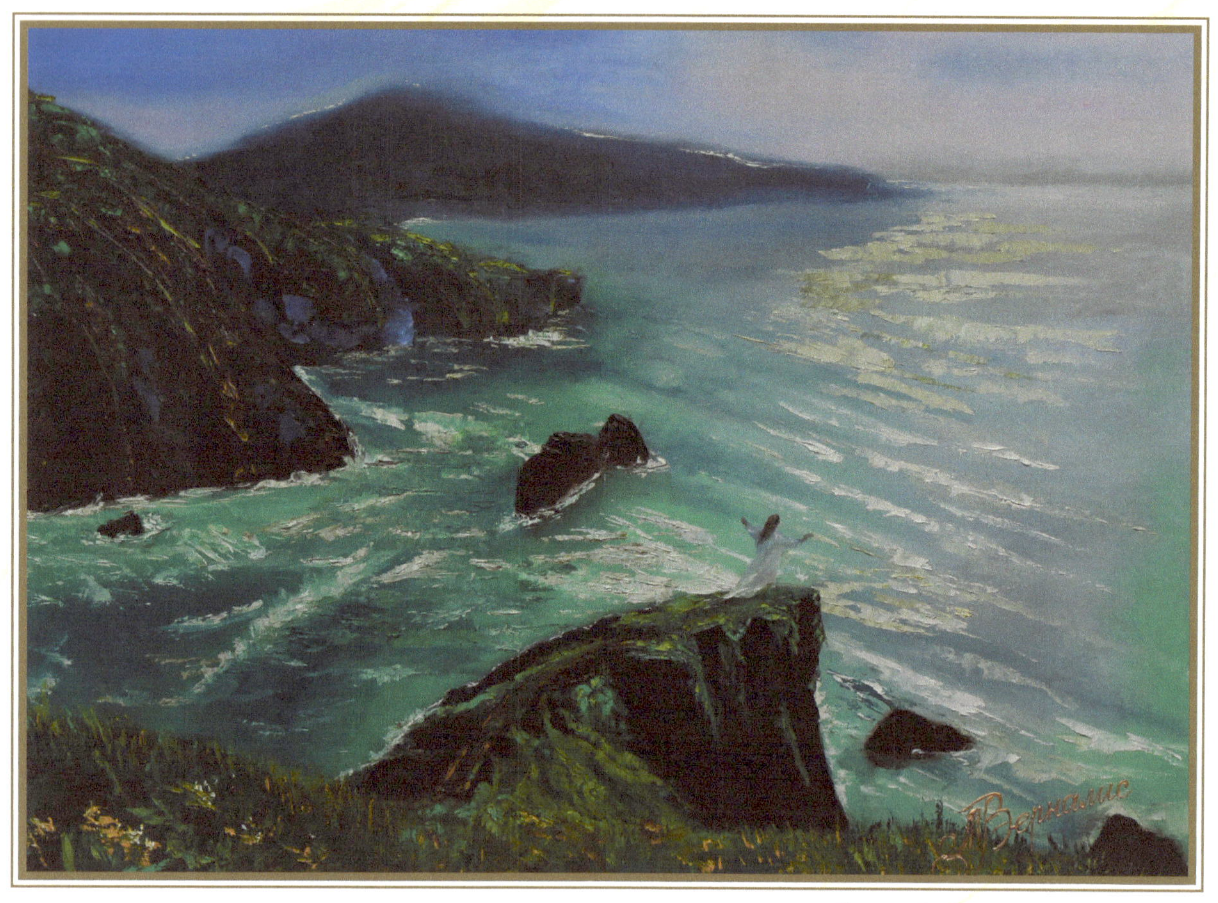

"Above the Sea" Oil, Canvas. 100x110

Huge mountains like wild beasts
The sea has quietened them only so it could tame them.
The sea has tamed them only to keep them calm!
To keep its peace!

I know that the sea dictates the waves.
Now it has its mercy, now it has its mercilessness.
Every conqueror of the sea is full of storms
And the faith to come back.

But every time it gives me its peace
Or rocking on the stormy waves,
It wants to conquer itself
And, forgetting the past, live in the present!

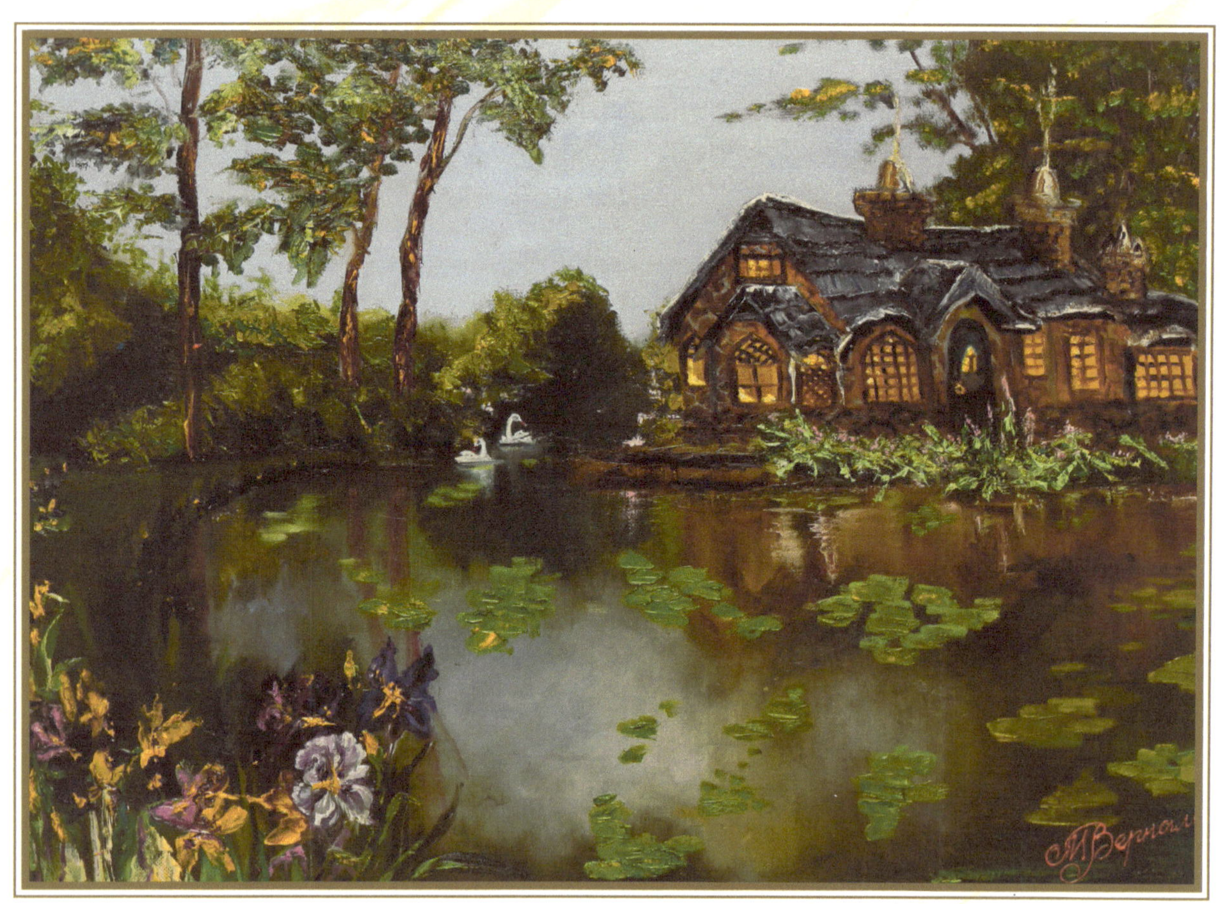

"A Little House For Two" Oil, Canvas 70x100 (Sold)

## TO UNDERSTAND ANOTHER PERSON

To understand another person is bliss!
After all, it's the greatest mystery of all!
Lovers, comrades, friends...
Who are you and I? Drawings with a pencil…

Our quiet home, with a gazebo in the courtyard,
With careless floral collages,
Where lilac bushes in bloom
Climbed up the wall!

To understand another man - no way!
They can't be understood, only accepted.
And at the door, a discreet bell
Warns that I am coming to you!

Our quiet home is cosy and beautiful,
It has a fireplace and a creaky couch
And like a restless neighbour
A magpie caws between the branches of the plum trees

To understand another man is nonsense!
What joy in that thankless toil?
To love! Then it is not difficult to understand,
And everything else is a long conversation...

Between the two of us, where our garden and home are,
Where the wind blows in the evening....
Where we are bound by mysterious ties
A spring day, asleep under the window!

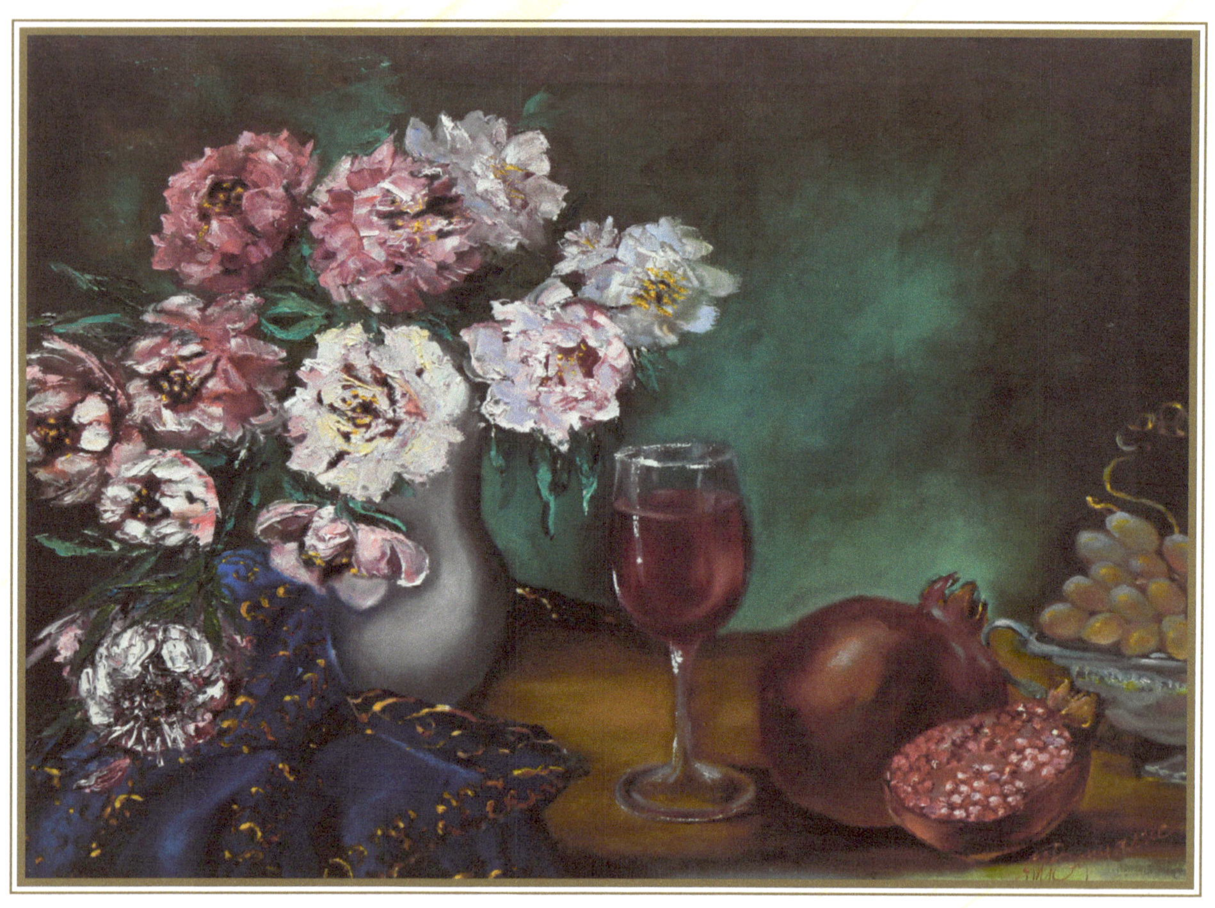

"Eastern Still-Life" Oil, Canvas, 80x100

How good it feels to be alone,
unbroken by a false bond
and realise that this happiness is
in the fireplace glowing with fire.

You and I will be alone
For beyond everything
We're made of one
Like the blue sky in your window

Fire will teach us to appreciate
The earthly coexistence
And how to replace our lust for possession
And to replace love with light

How good it is for the two of us
to be destined for good fortune.
I hide daisies between the pages,
that were our calendar...

How good it is to be together...

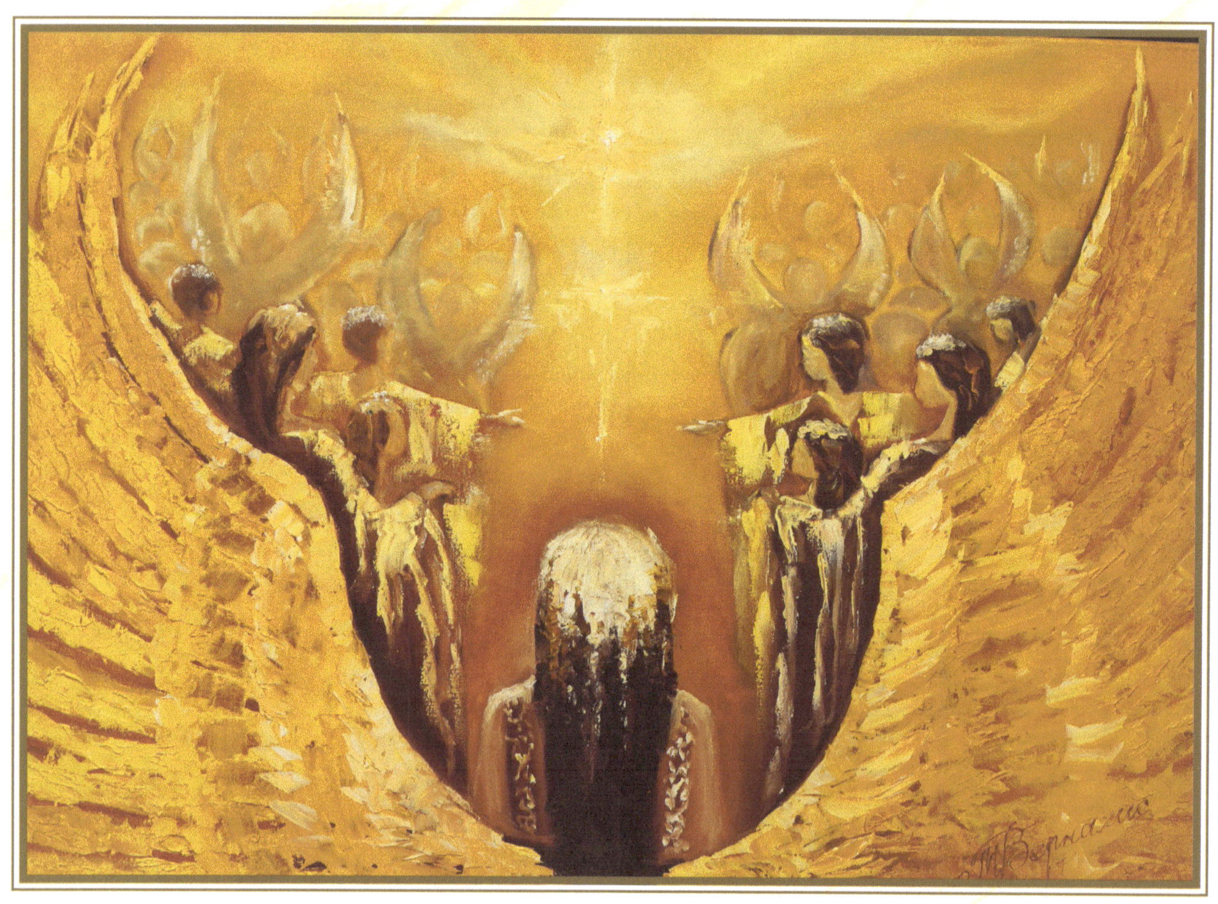

"City Of Angels" Oil, Canvas. 70x100 (Sold)

God only created Light. The soul is Light!
There is nothing other than Light.
And the sun has been shining for millions of years...
But how can the soul understand it all?

One cannot appreciate warmth without coldness,
When you don't see sorrow you don't know happiness.
When there is no evil, what is good?
When there is no whole, what is there to divide into parts?

So the soul may see its light,
God surrounds it with darkness,
And whether to fear the darkness or not,
That's for each man to decide.

One thing is certain, in the darkness
Don't curse the absence of the Light
Don't be angry and don't make threats! It is for you
To see your Light and be given it all!

Remain a Light in the gloom!
Know yourself as God knows you!
Stay true to yourself -
God only sends angels to meet you!

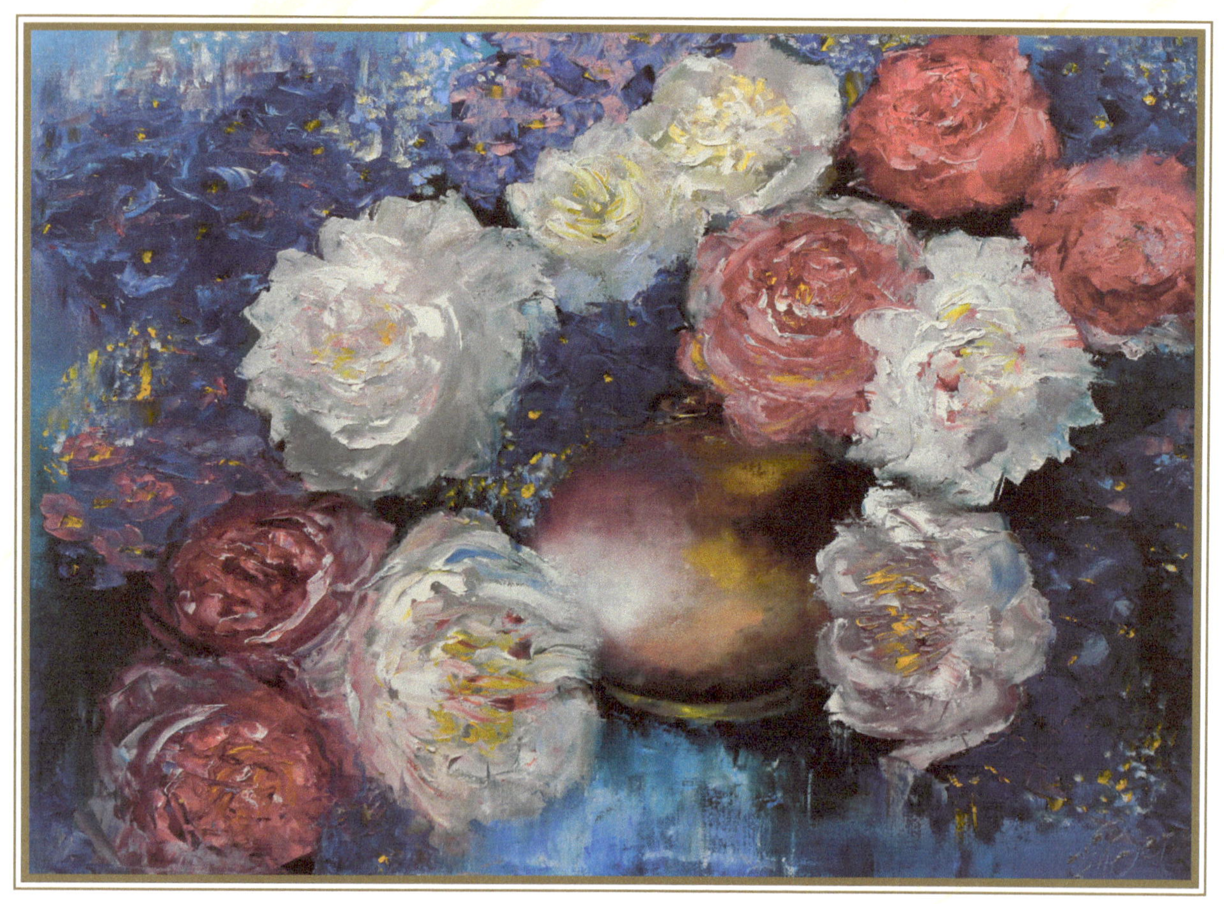

"The Scent Of Peonies" Oil, Canvas. 70x100 (Sold)

## RONDO IN SUMMER STYLE

Like a red-hot balloon, the day rolls on into the sunset,
All the grasses in the weary meadows are crushed.
And the thunder in the heavens is but the first payment
for happiness... The thunder has a frightful sound!

The night is poured into the glass with summer's heady tincture.
I proclaim a toast! In the clear blue
Forest silence is fresh, half-dressed:
Tunics of cobwebs quiver on high...

The night gloom is intoxicating... Fog diluted with dew,
The pre-dawn blue hangs over the earth...
Walk barefoot on the silk grass
Cut up the dawn's light with a scythe...

Like a glowing ball, the day rolls on to sunset!

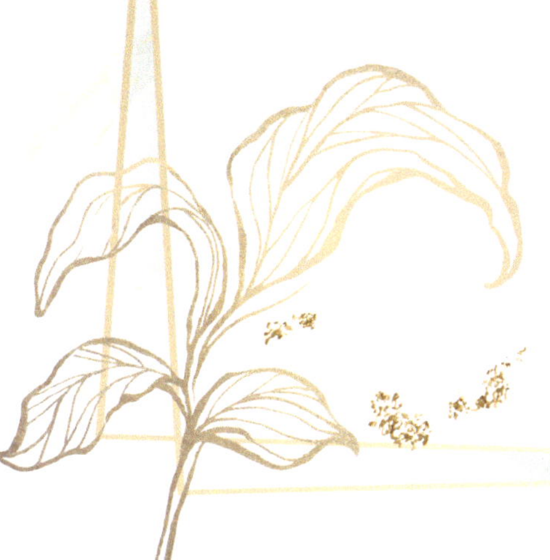

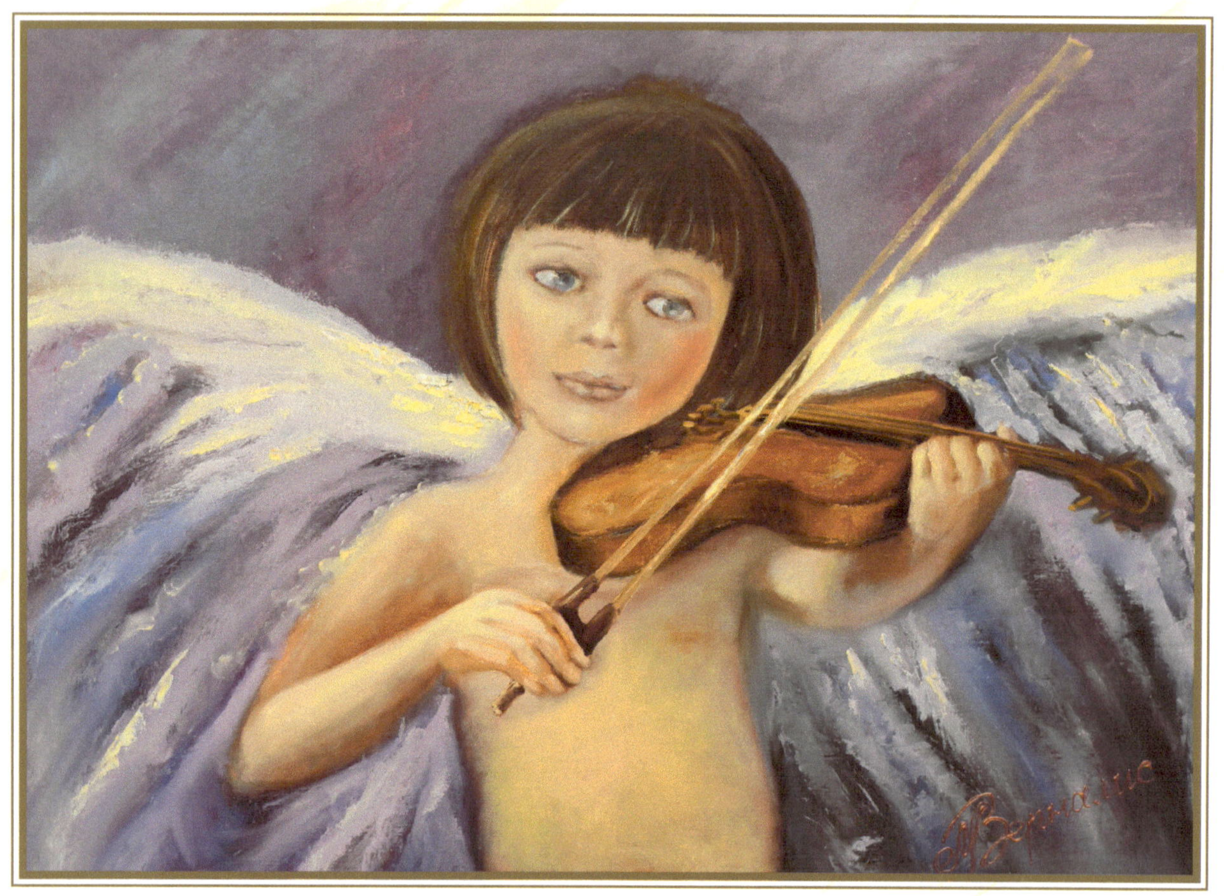

"Angel" Oil, Canvas. 70x100

My white-winged angel, my Muse,
You are my inspiration!
My way is the fruit of our union.
I thank you for this

For appearing in the evening
When the hum of the day fades
And putting your wings on my shoulders
And talking to me

About wonders and distant lands
that I should hold my ground!
Which, strange as it may seem,
Is a chance to be myself!

And if angel wings
Were given by fate,
There's no room for thoughts of powerlessness!
I can do anything. God is with me!

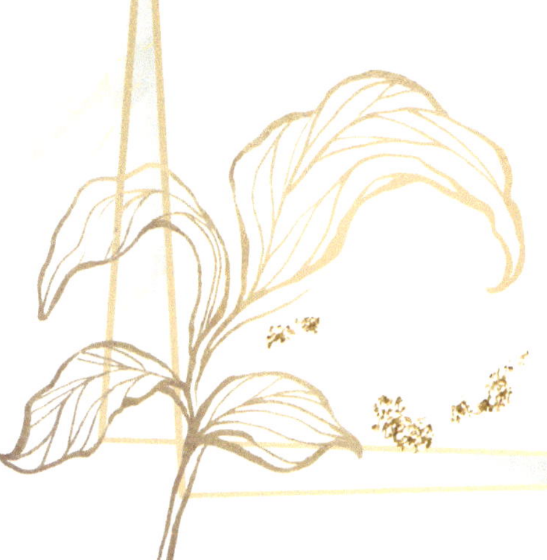

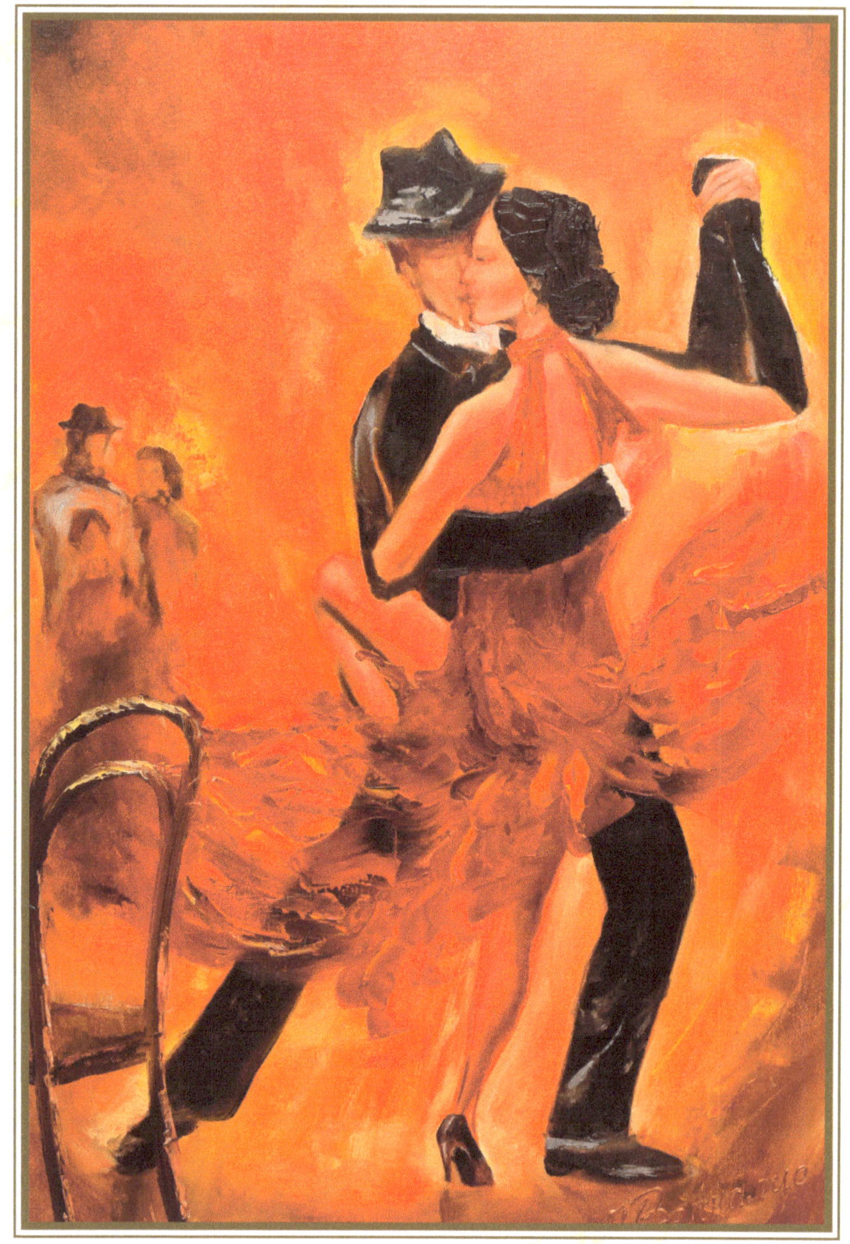

"Tango" Oil, Canvas, 60x80

**OUR LOVE'S TANGO!**

The tango of our love sounds
With the same passion as the first time!
It's a powerful tune
The happiness in a lover's eye!

The tango of our love
Two open wings that flap!
It's a powerful tune
The passion of the south winds!

Tango! I'm captivated by your tender hands...
Tango! The dance of meeting through the pain of separation!
True, we've found each other...
The tango is the dance of our love!

The tango of a shooting star
And the midnight avenue is hushed...
The city is asleep. Just me and you.
This dance is our white verse.

The harmony of two hearts
The lightness of feeling and movement!
A circle of hands, a circle of two rings!
Tango, the dance of trust!

Tango! I'm captivated by your gentle hands...
Tango! The dance of meeting through the pain of separation!
True, we've found each other
The tango is the dance of our love!

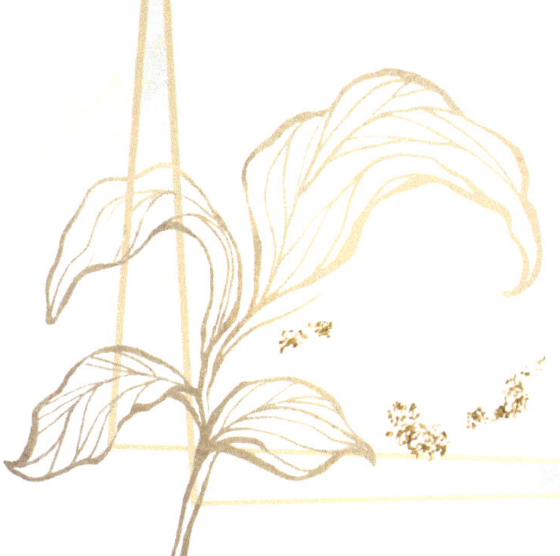

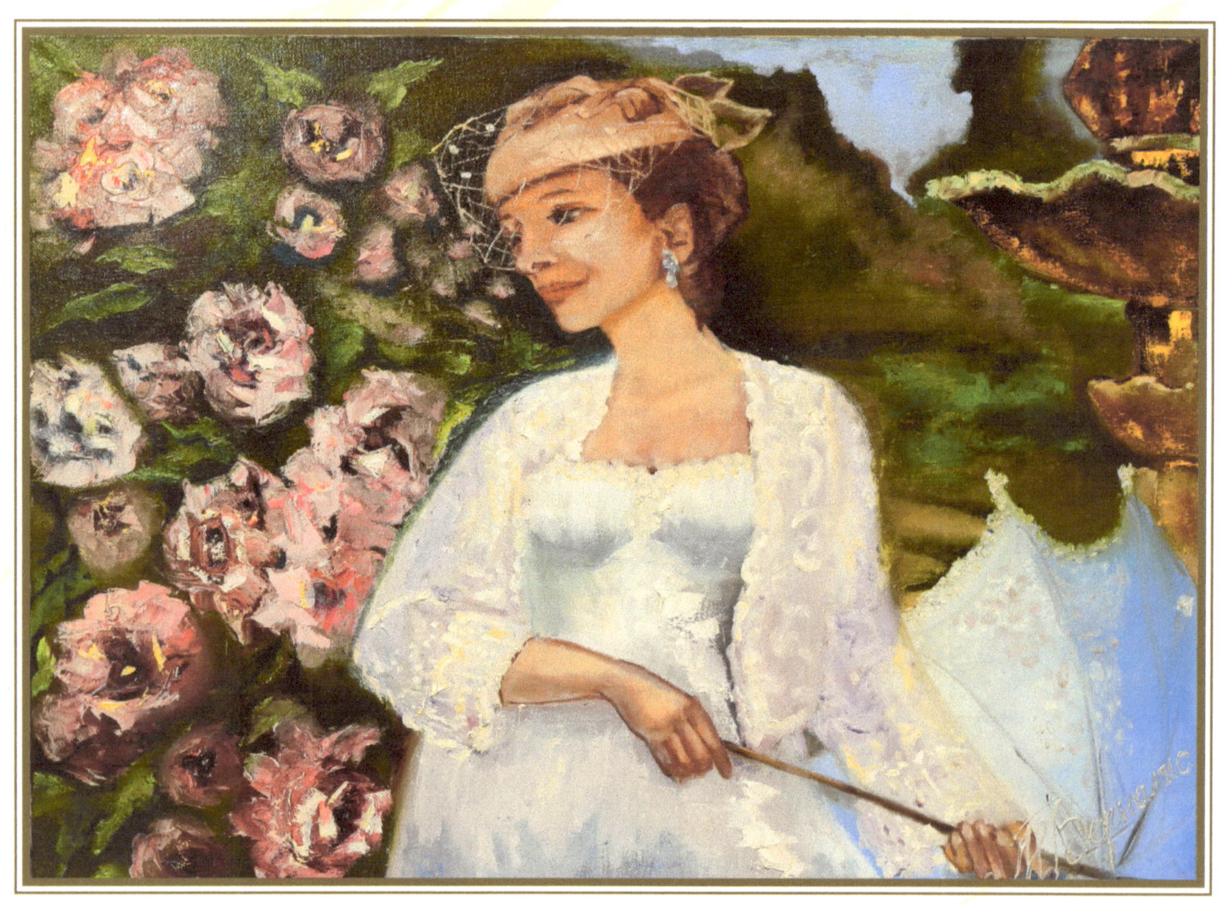

"A Walk in The Springtime" Oil, Canvas, 70x100

## MEMORIES OF THE PERINALDO

I walked as if I were remembering
And I recognised every house.
As if I had been here before
Or lived in it once.
And these stones underfoot,
And these frescoes on the wall
Were like words I had once heard,
As if related to me.
And I listened even
To the native rustling of the winds
And the tower that stands guard
The history of five centuries...
And I lingered till sundown,
For fear of not remembering without it,
Was I born here?
In what century? For what purpose?
And my tears of light
Are, in fact, the answer:
I was born here for Love,
To be a poet in this life!

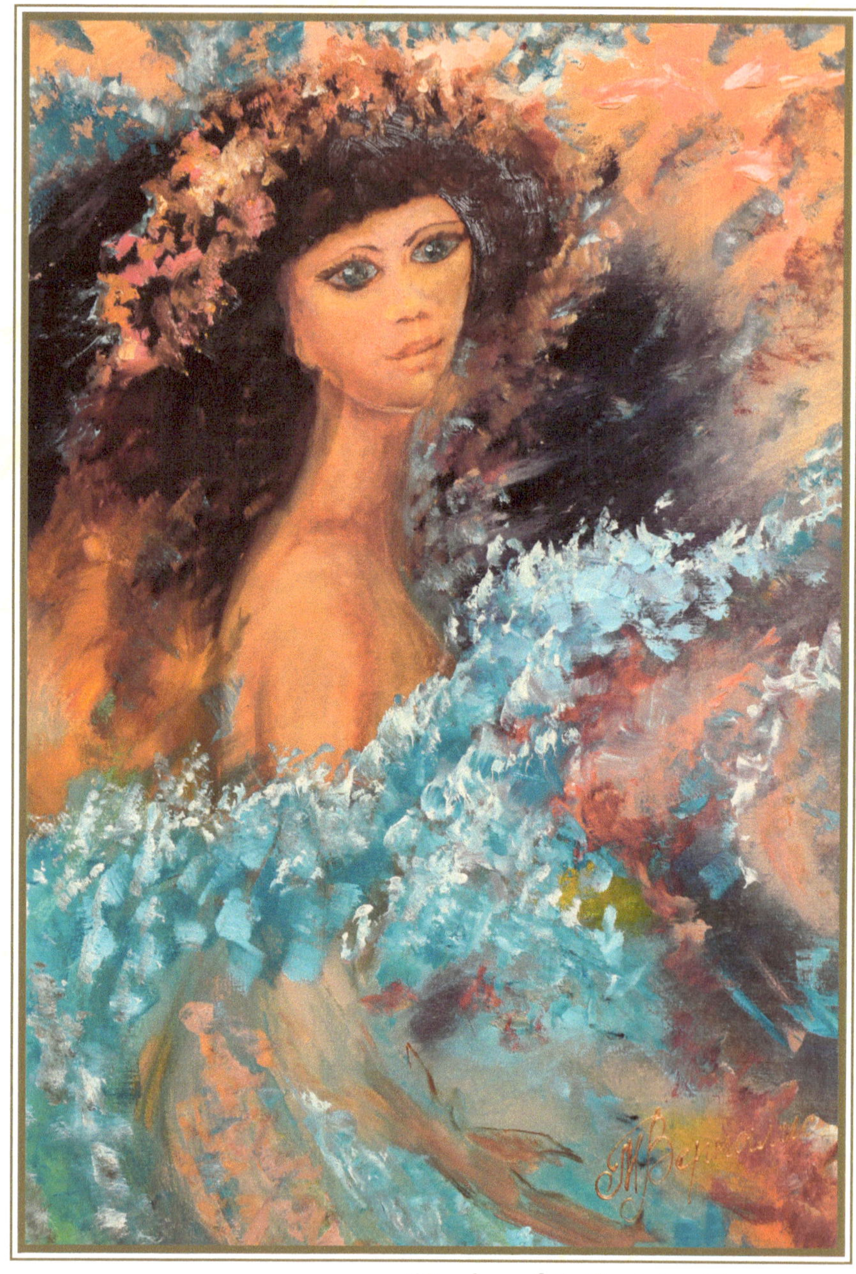

"Condition of the Soul" Oil, Canvas. 60x90

It's a kind of a riddle,
Kind of a craving for goodness -
Thoughts are in complete delirium,
My heart's in complete delirium...

I walk along the sea
Where the sun sets
And the waves are coming towards me
With pebbles the waves rush towards me

Maybe it's the eve
Of new encounters and sweet friendships
Or maybe it's just disbelief
That you are a stranger in my heart

Maybe it's the oblivion
Of old tensions and old grudges
Or obedience
That speaks in me?

What is the condition
That once more rules my senses?
Is it the thought of farewell,
Or is it love again...?

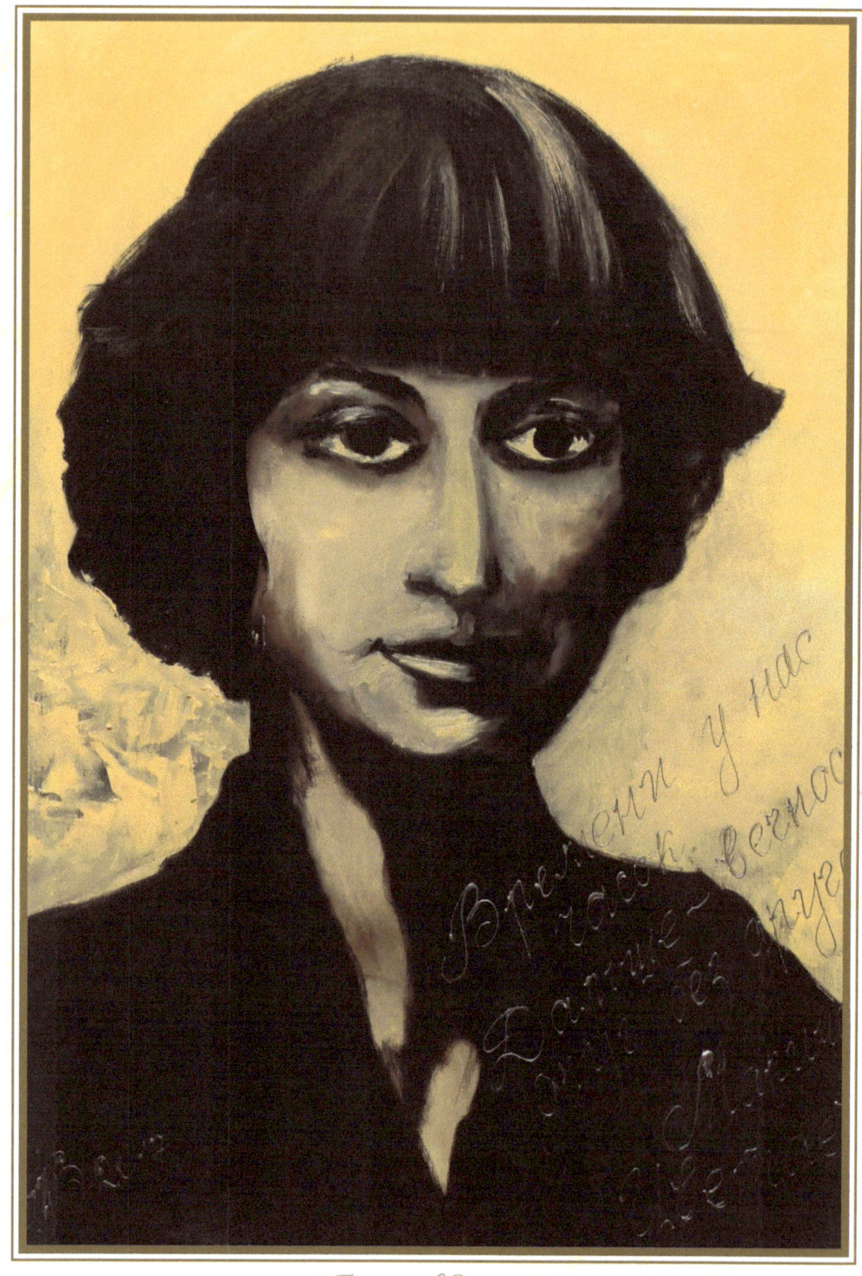

"Portrait of Marina Tsvetaeva" Oil, Canvas. 60x80

## A DEDICATION TO MARINA TSVETAEVA

*(On the day when her sister, Anastasia Tsvetaeva, passed away)*

And they will have something to talk about,
To meet for ever in a new world.
To be together and forget the decay of bodies.
And a whole century to paint on Marina's face!

A century without her green eyes
Where the sound of the tambourine is forgotten
Where the bolero is overshadowed by carefree jazz,
Where her mountain ash still burns!

She has so much to say
That the wines of her poems are intoxicating!
A century later, her album
So full of sentiment, so full of love and so alluring

The creations of immeasurable heights,
To a depth that no one can reach!
When she's gone, you're left...
A soul comes true! Why stay?

When you come to her with a claim of faith,
Tell her who got the wolf's fur,
That a century, like her, who knew no measure,
Worships her, one of all!

Dear Marina! The ringing of Moscow
My sister carries in her hands.
The cathedral of the Virgin Mary sends her greetings to you
And the doves flying in the sky.

I know that time will not blow away my memory.
I wander through the seven halls of the Kremlin.
And kiss you goodbye in my bosom
Moscow, my dear city!

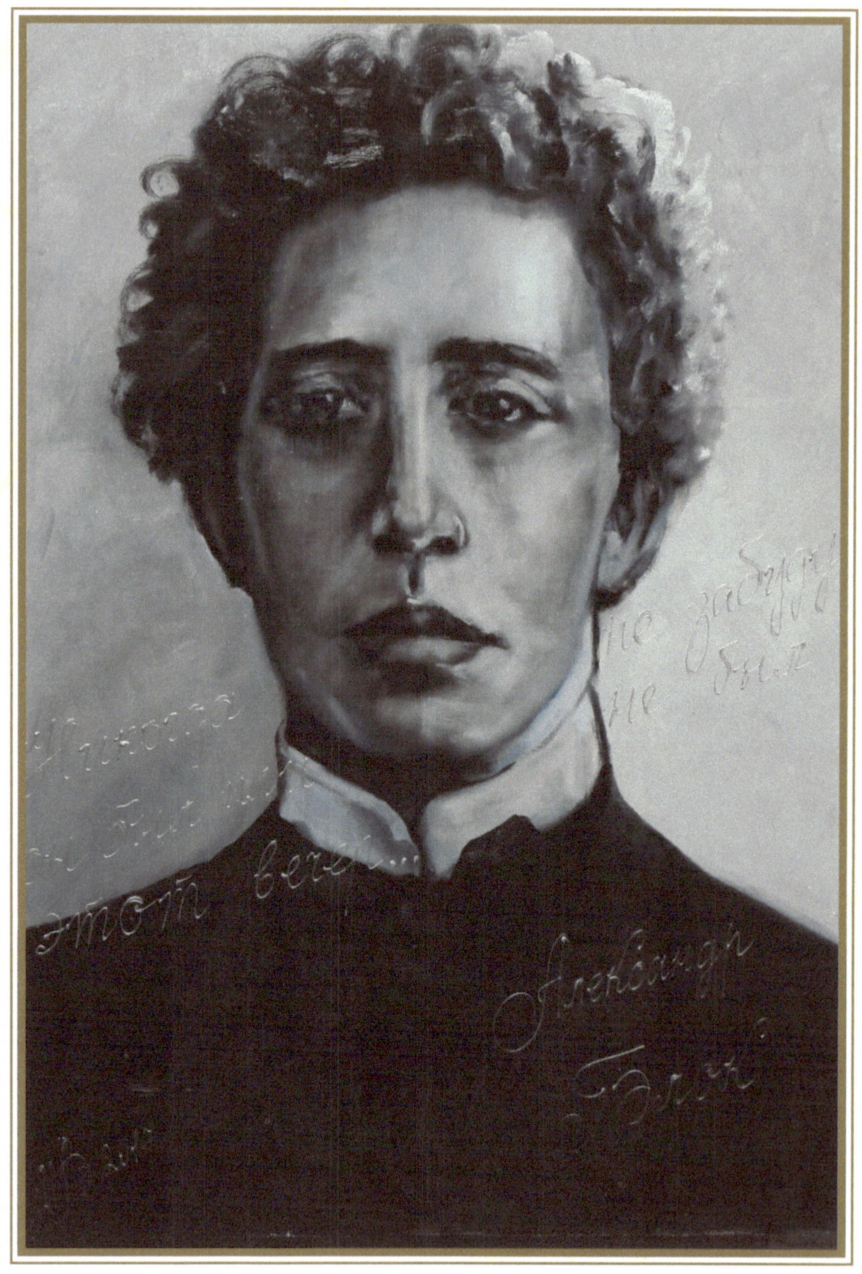


"Alexander Blok Portrait" Oil, Canvas. 60x80

A blank page! It is so obedient
To the bold strokes of his pen.
He's generous to all
To all those with whom he has met
Of inspiration or sorrow
Or the new rise of a dream,
A clean slate, I notice,
Clean not from emptiness,
But the soon to be born
On the unseen lines
Of a new creation.
(even if it is still but a draft!)
A clean slate. How important it is
All that's past, is to be discarded
And to feel one day
The path to follow from now on.
And like a line on paper
Step by step on paper,
To realise in the last step,
To take a silent look...
From the brass knob of the study
To the bindings of the window.
Such is the poet's fate:
A clean slate... and the thoughts soar!

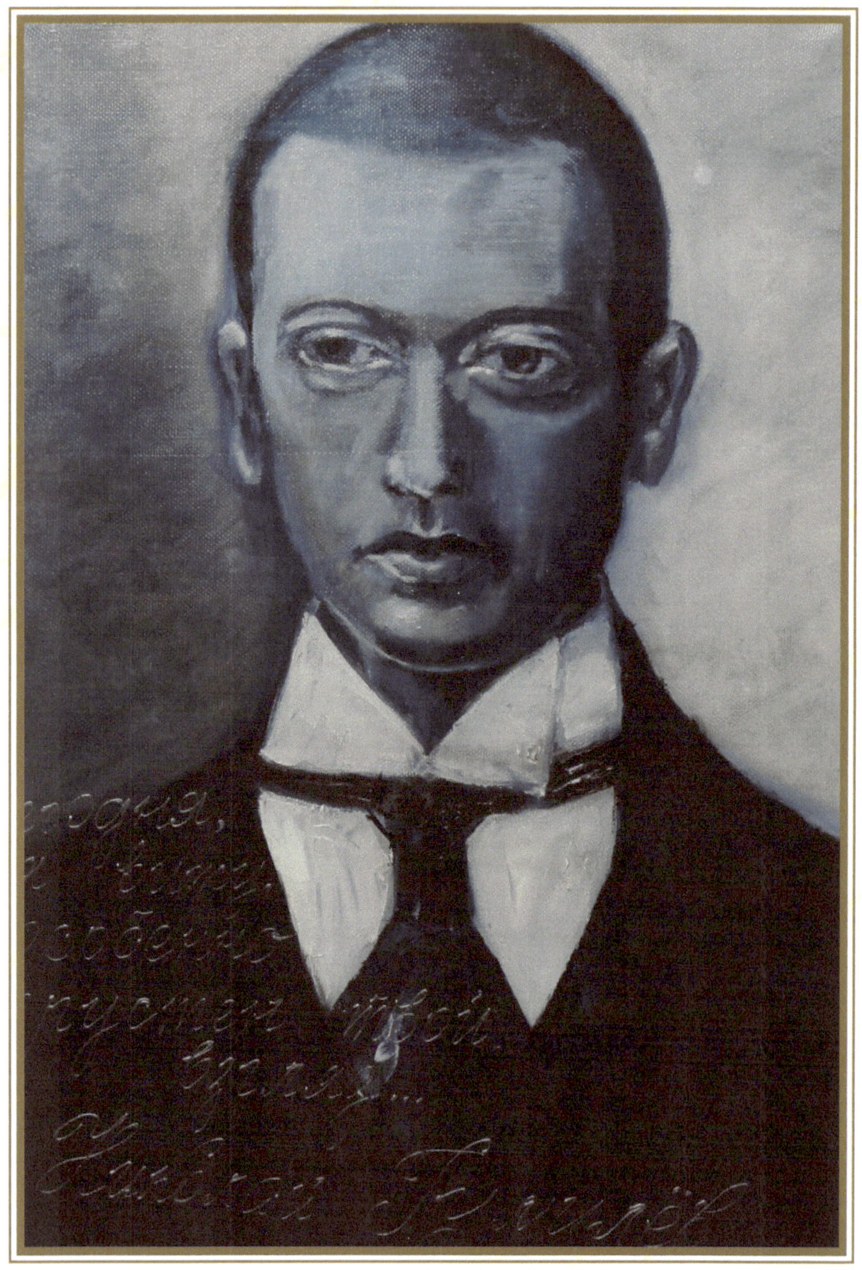

*"Nikolai Gumilev Portrait" Oil, Canvas. 60x80*

## THE PARABLE OF THE CRICKET

Two friends in the hustle and bustle of the big city
One day they met by chance.
One appreciated the taste of city life,
The other loved his countryside!

And, treasuring the moment of their encounter,
The two friends began their conversation.
Though their speeches were drowned in the noise of the city...
They couldn't keep silent!

The village man, in the heat of the conversation
Could not hide his astonishment.
And he whispered softly to the other:
Listen! There seems to be a cricket here!

How could he hear it in all that noise?
Crickets are fainter than the rumble of cars!
He went over and raked the grass with his hands
And he smiled: It's not just one!

There's a whole choir of them! Listen to them chirping!
His friend from the town was amazed.
And he took his coins and threw them... By the curb
The familiar sound was heard.

At the sound of the coins people turned around
In their hurry to check their wallets
They heard it and smiled in embarrassment,
As if to apologise: "It's not mine"

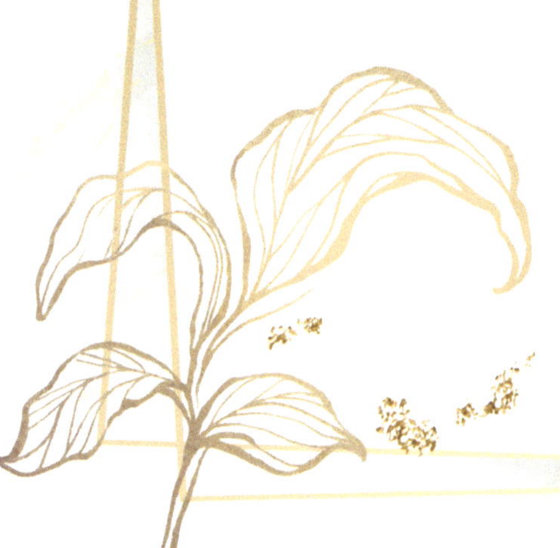

They looked at each other in silence,
For the truth turned out to be simple:
Everyone hears what he wants to hear.
The sound that the soul is attuned to!

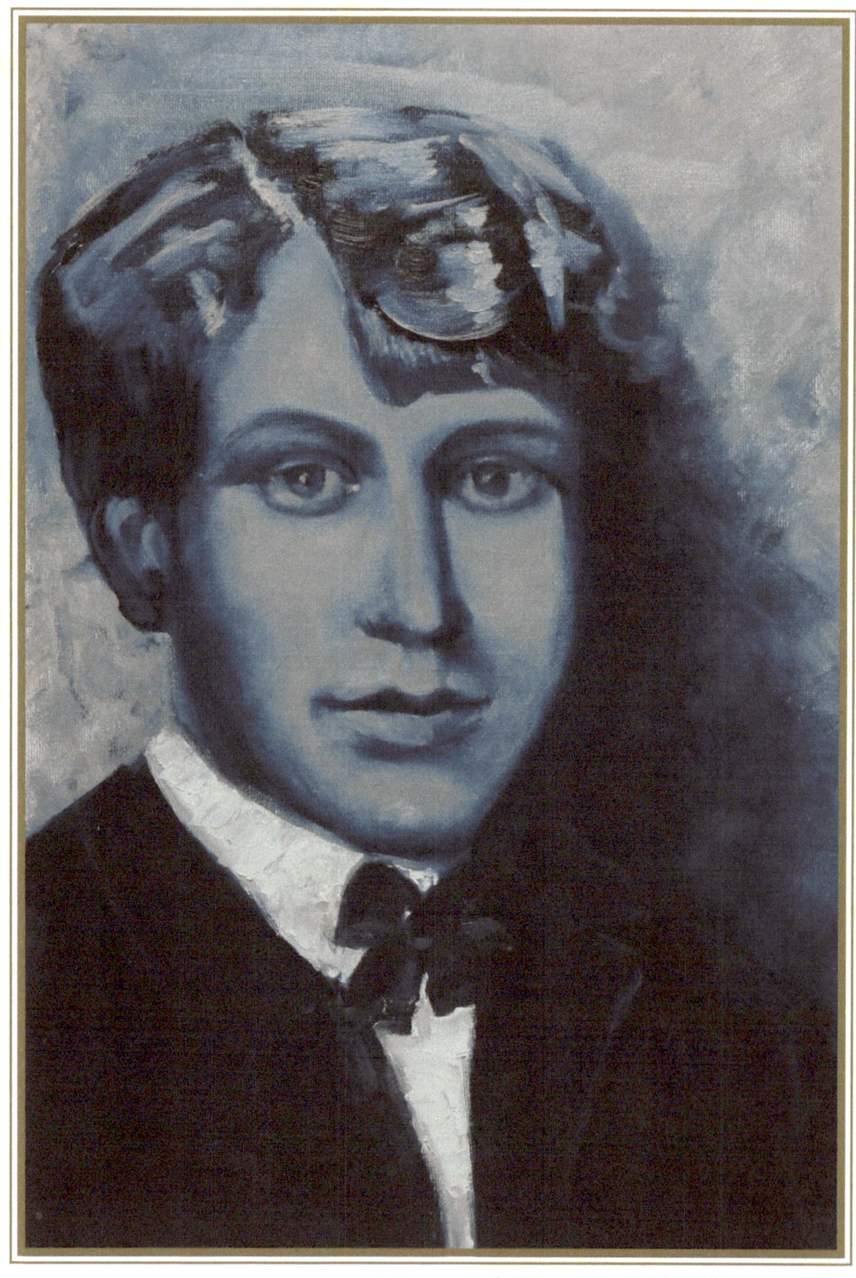

"Portrait Of Sergei Esenin" Oil, Canvas. 60x80

Poems are born from silence,
From the light haze of a windy syllable,
From that eloquent mute,
Which solemnly and sternly

That first line in the notebook,
Smoothing out thought with the palm of its rhyme.
And everyone knows the grace
That eternity, too, has algorithms:

The light of day replaces night, and life is faithful
To the law of conservation of energy.
Where the peak of the beginning of feeling is silence!
And personality is the bridge between the stars and thorns.

Poems are born from silence,
From that tinkling subtlety of space,
From whence we all came into this world,
Followed by the law of permanence!

God guides us! And in the silence of the poems
We taste the life-giving moisture
Of those precious foundations of life
Wherein lie strength and courage!

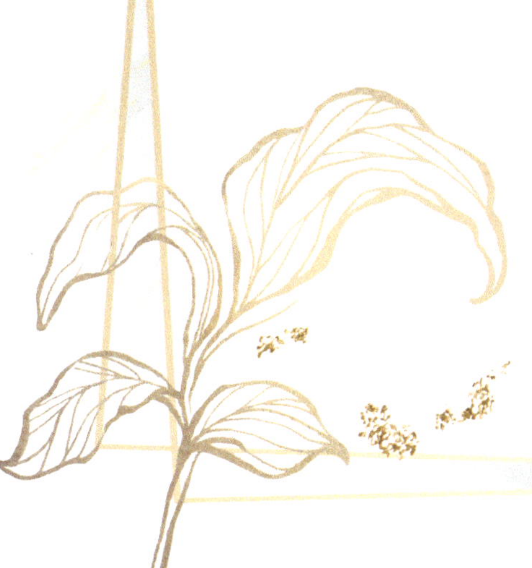

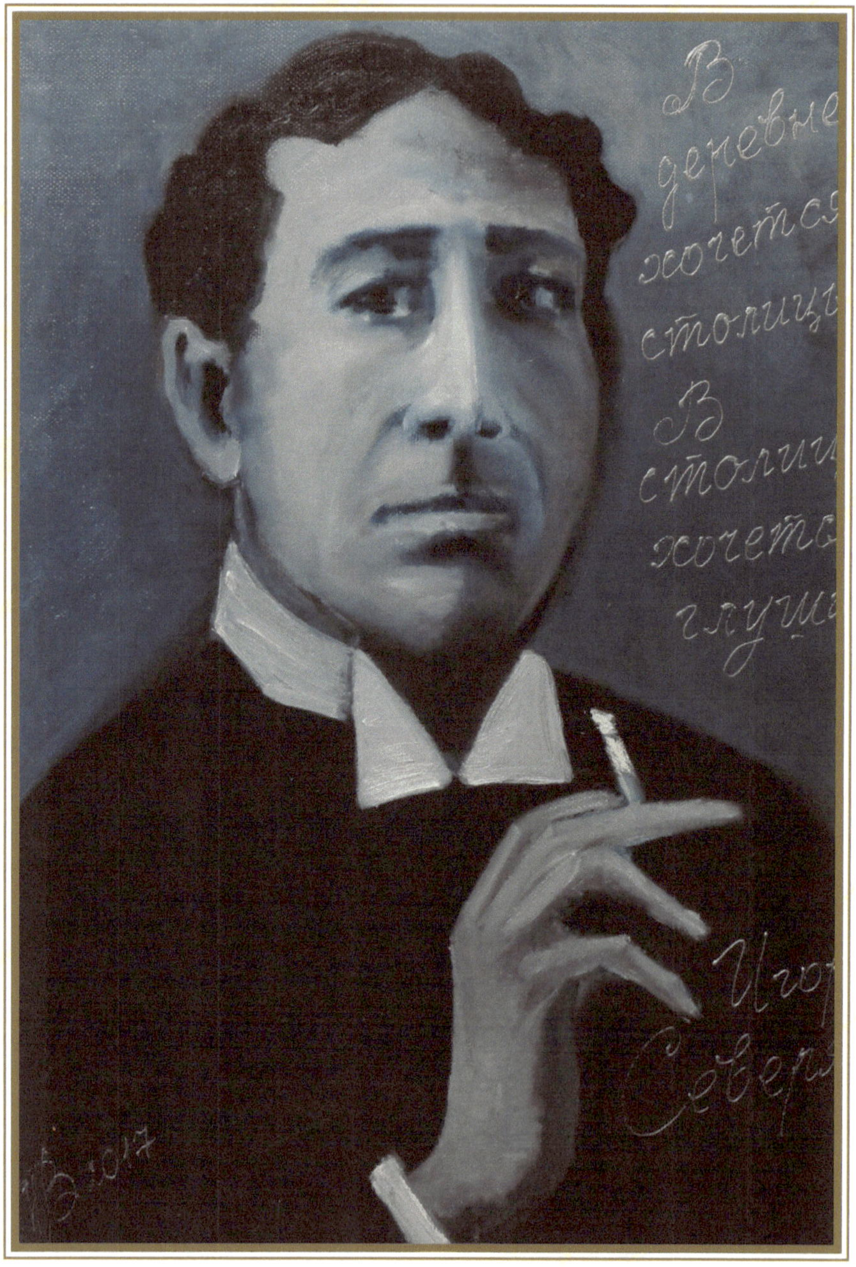


"Igor Severyanin Portrait" Oil, Canvas. 60x80

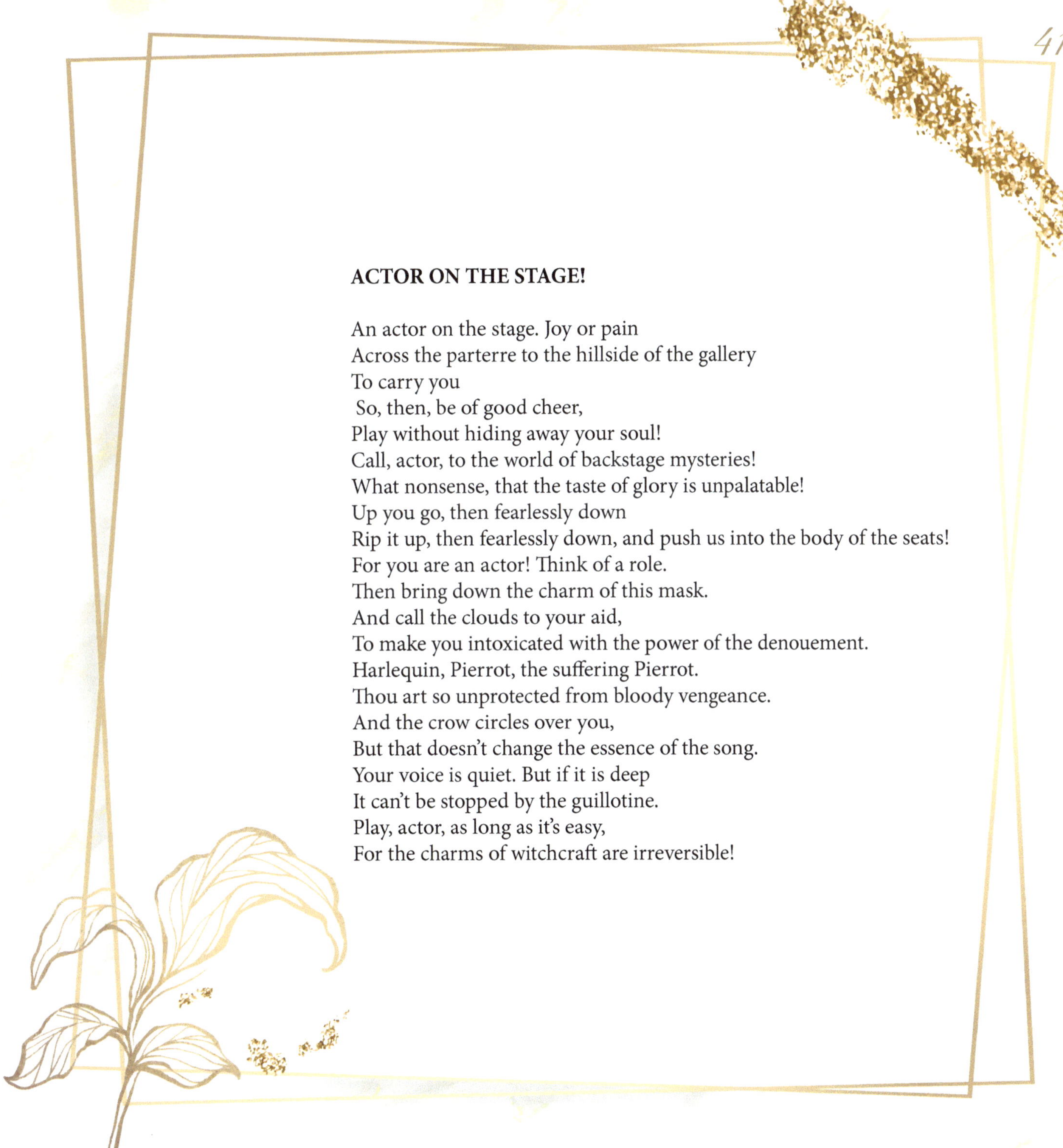

**ACTOR ON THE STAGE!**

An actor on the stage. Joy or pain
Across the parterre to the hillside of the gallery
To carry you
So, then, be of good cheer,
Play without hiding away your soul!
Call, actor, to the world of backstage mysteries!
What nonsense, that the taste of glory is unpalatable!
Up you go, then fearlessly down
Rip it up, then fearlessly down, and push us into the body of the seats!
For you are an actor! Think of a role.
Then bring down the charm of this mask.
And call the clouds to your aid,
To make you intoxicated with the power of the denouement.
Harlequin, Pierrot, the suffering Pierrot.
Thou art so unprotected from bloody vengeance.
And the crow circles over you,
But that doesn't change the essence of the song.
Your voice is quiet. But if it is deep
It can't be stopped by the guillotine.
Play, actor, as long as it's easy,
For the charms of witchcraft are irreversible!

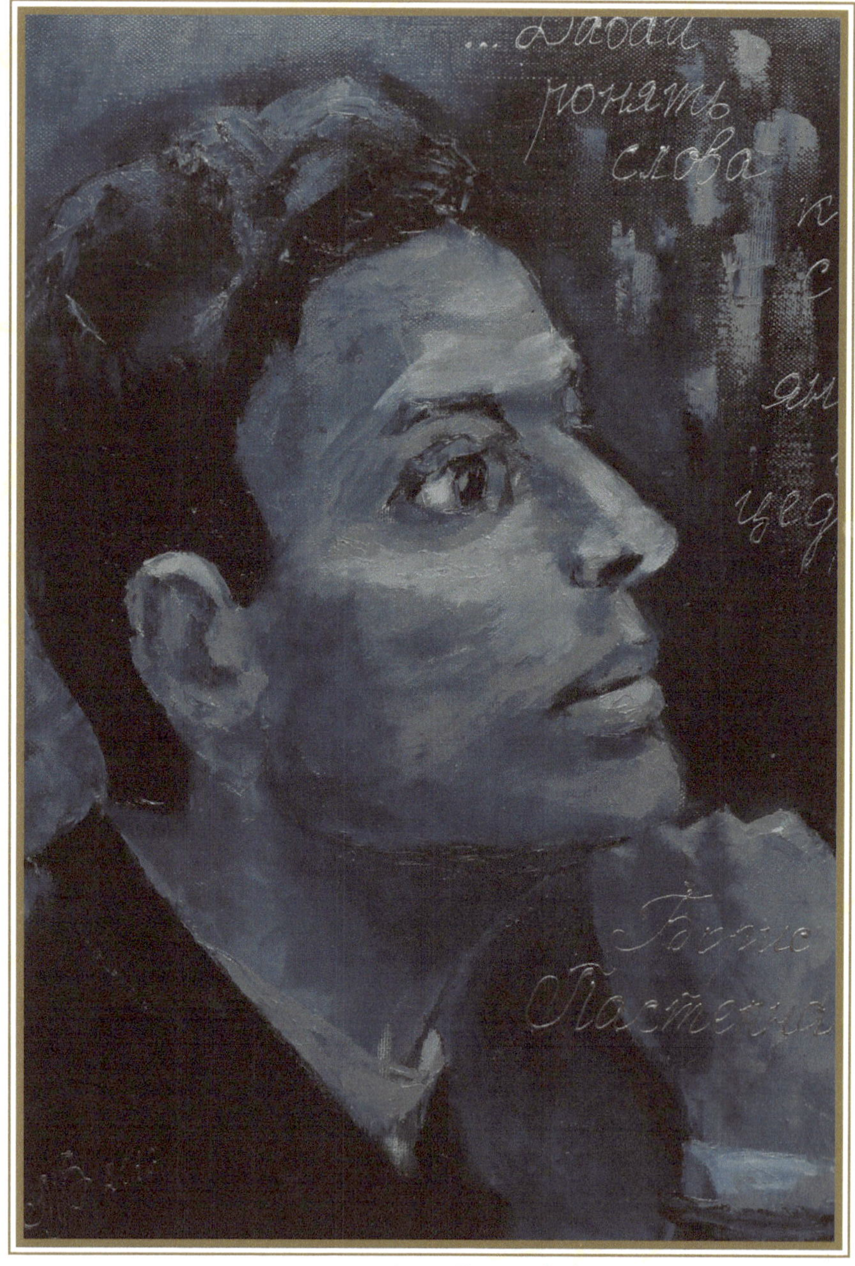


"Boris Pasternak Portrait" Oil, Canvas. 60x80

Lead me, I'm an apprentice again
I'm going camping again
To be separated from the comforts of home,
To realise that it's the other way round,

That constancy is called the moment,
The moment is eternity and the dream is reality,
That happiness is never immutable,
But you can't fix it!

Lead me on, I heed your words,
I'm trying to understand and reason
As in the Bible I forgive my enemies
I try to love my neighbour.

My desk is a shrine to me.
Poems and watercolours and blue
Leading me to a new peak
And I honour my desk as a sacred thing, and here the poems
And the watercolours and the blue lead me to new heights.

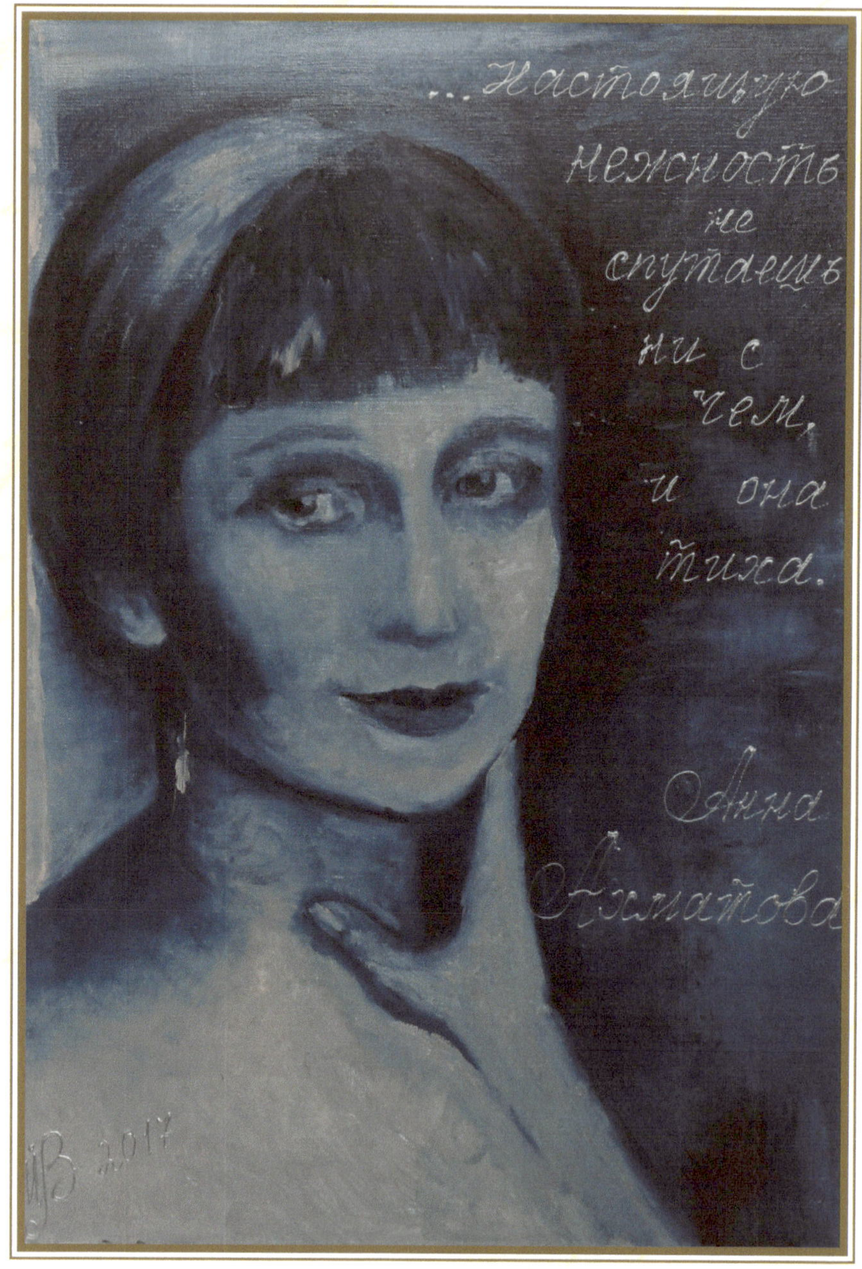


*"Anna Akhmatova Poirtrait" Oil, Canvas. 60x80*

**BELIEF**

You kiss the top of my head in silence...
And you hold me in your arms as if guarding me!
Dawn is looking at my pillow,
Where you still lie in your happy sleep!

Every moment is precious
Of two people's blissful embrace
That my eyelids are warmly closed
And in my sleep I touch them with my lips.

I'll feel your tenderness spread
And my head against your chest...
Trust gives birth to serenity
Of touch and love's fire!

I wouldn't change a freckle of you
With you I am happy in rain and snow
And in your dreams, kiss me on the top of my head!
I'm the happiest in those moments, believe me!

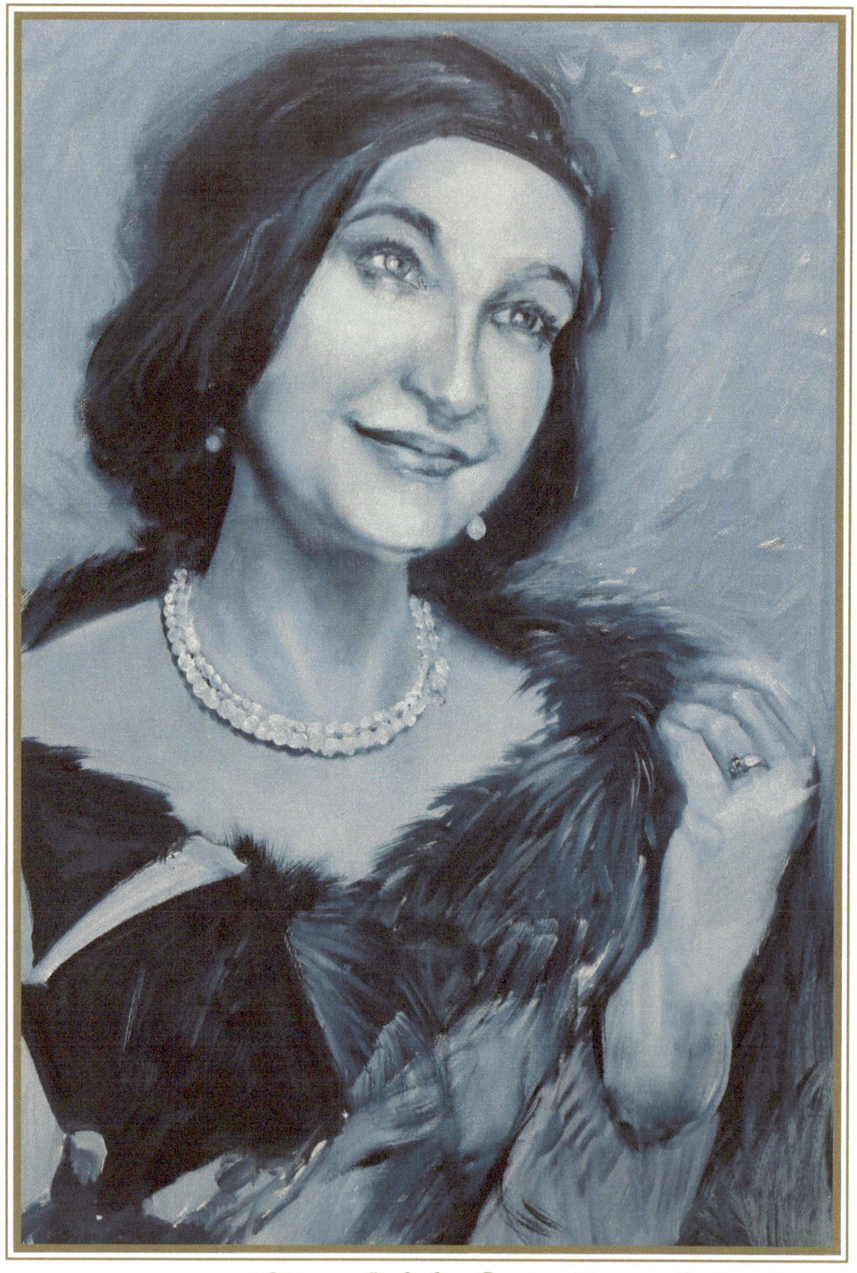

"Marina Shkrobova-Vernalis Portrait" by Alina Olenina"
Oil, Canvas. 60x80

**TO BE A WOMAN!**

To be a woman is bliss and longing,
War and peace, work and art.
To be the fluttering autumn leaf,
Giving the most naive feeling

A moment! And the wind will blow
Your golden charm,
But remember how tenderly the leaf will cling
To the giver of a drop of peace,

To him who, with his shoulder behind you,
Knows how to admire beauty.
(Ah, maybe all this has nothing to do with it),
But it's so good to be yourself.

Funny and weak, a silent brook,
Filled with magical water,
Which, when you approach in secret,
I know I can't help myself!

To be a woman is anxiety and comfort,
All masks of lines dear to the heart.
To be the one who has been waited on for half a century,
To come like an unexpected summer downpour!

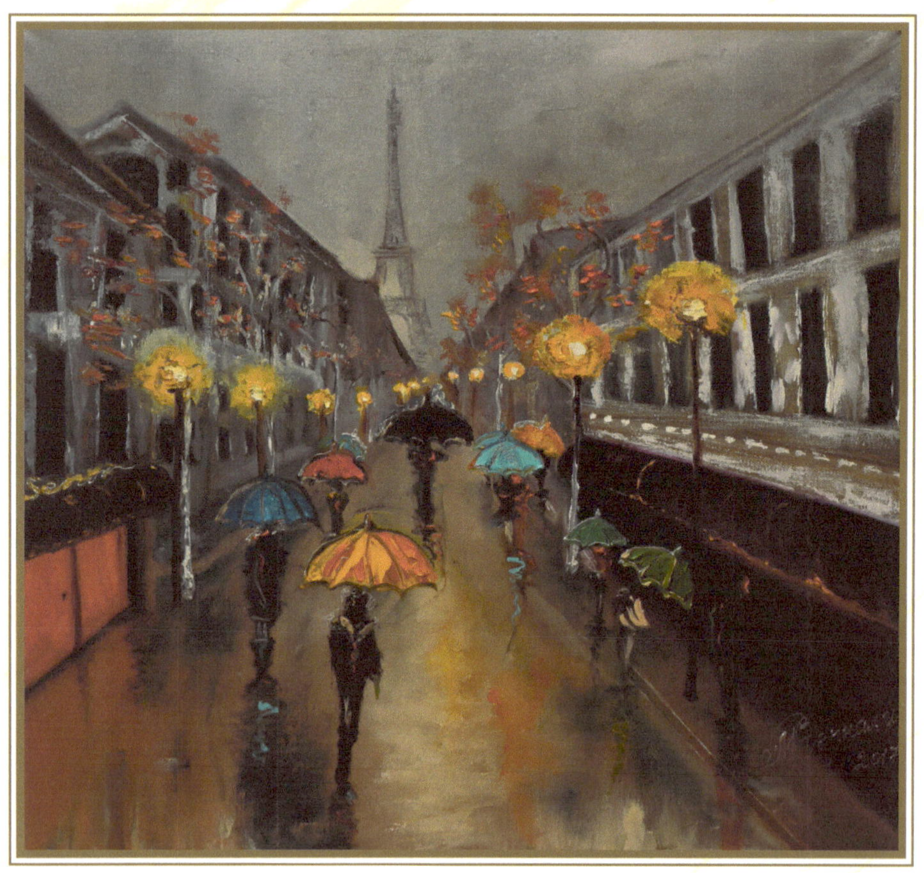

"Rain Over Paris" Oil, Canvas, 100x100

**DARE! J`AI OSE!!!**

The rains over Paris are lower and lower
And in the mist the Sacré Coeur is gone.
And heavy drops fall from the roof
The Parisian temper!

The rains over Paris, now louder, now quieter
Through the Concord Square!
The sun god of Egypt seems to hear
The drenched people of Paris!

Rains over Paris on the tops of umbrellas
Over the Champs-Élysées...
In the hope that someone might hear
The call: "J`ai ose!" "J`ai ose!"

Rains over Paris, dare to go higher!
Be equal to your dream!
Then God will hear our desires
And will say to himself, "J`ai ose!"

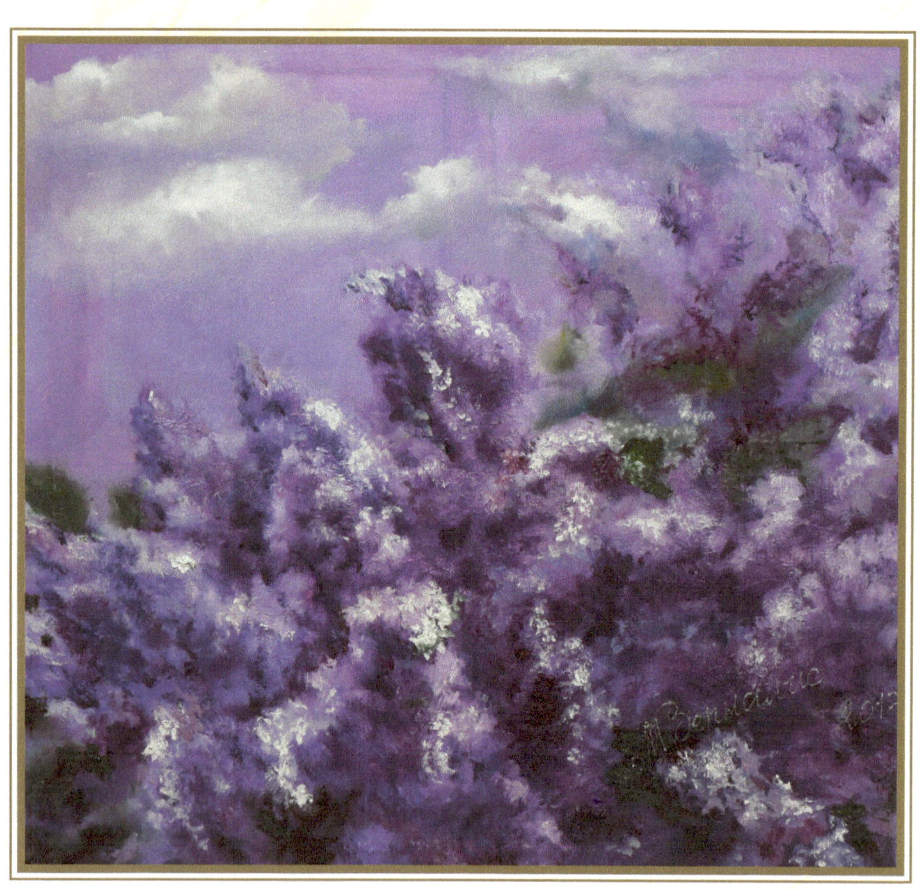

"Lilac Clouds" Oil, Canvas. 90x90 (Sold)

**UMBRELLAS**

Umbrellas like little bats
Heads down on the wall.
We sat there, hardly breathing...
He kept hugging my knees!

Afterwards, in spite of our tired heads,
We hid in the green, among the decrepit buildings,
And a bunch of soggy lilacs
And held out a bunch of the lilacs in exchange for empty confessions...

And then the two of us, in the fresh puddles
Walked, forgetting the umbrellas on the wall.
And spring's stray cold
Ran a shiver through my knees!

I've been fond of any frost ever since
And inky lilac beds
And the day before yesterday he became my husband
Just for hugging my knees!

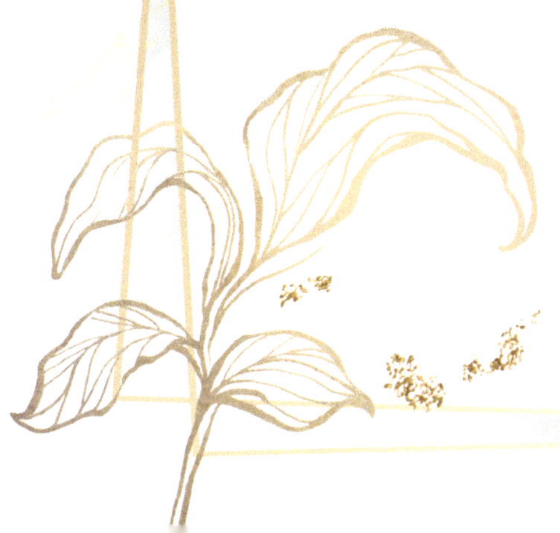

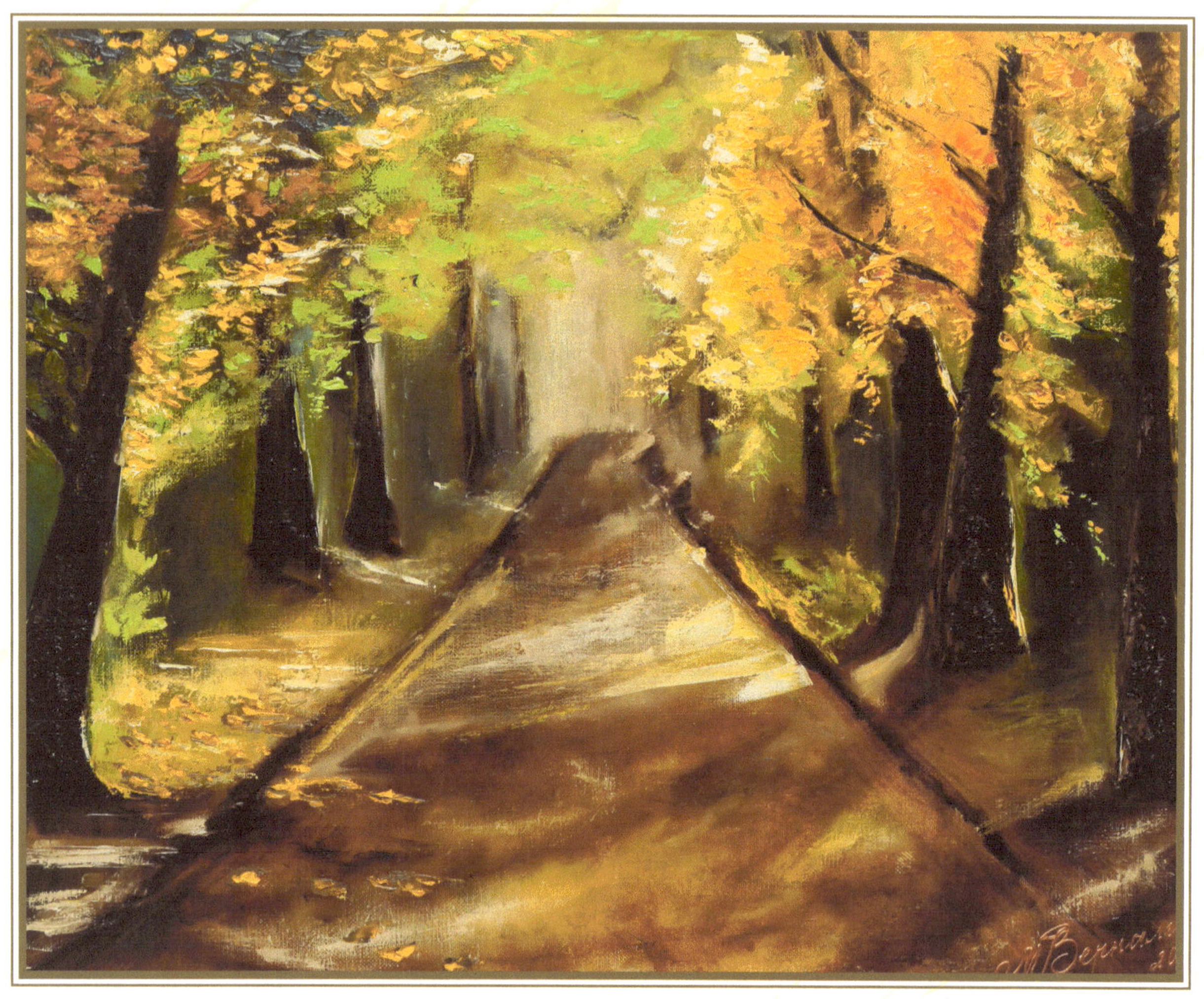

"Autumn Alley" Oil, Canvas. 70x100

What have we done to deserve such an autumn?!
There must be a reckoning!
And if we ask Heaven about it,
It'll say: To show you

All the colours of the forest, all the tenderness of feeling
And the dance of the leaves that dance at the ball!
For all who rush to the point of folly,
For all those who are tired of believing and living:

For all who look around and look back
And look out the window of their souls!
To see the faces and not hurry,
To see faces and not hurry...

What have we done to deserve such an autumn?!
It's Heaven's generosity!
We always get what we ask for
In the strength of the faith of those who asked!

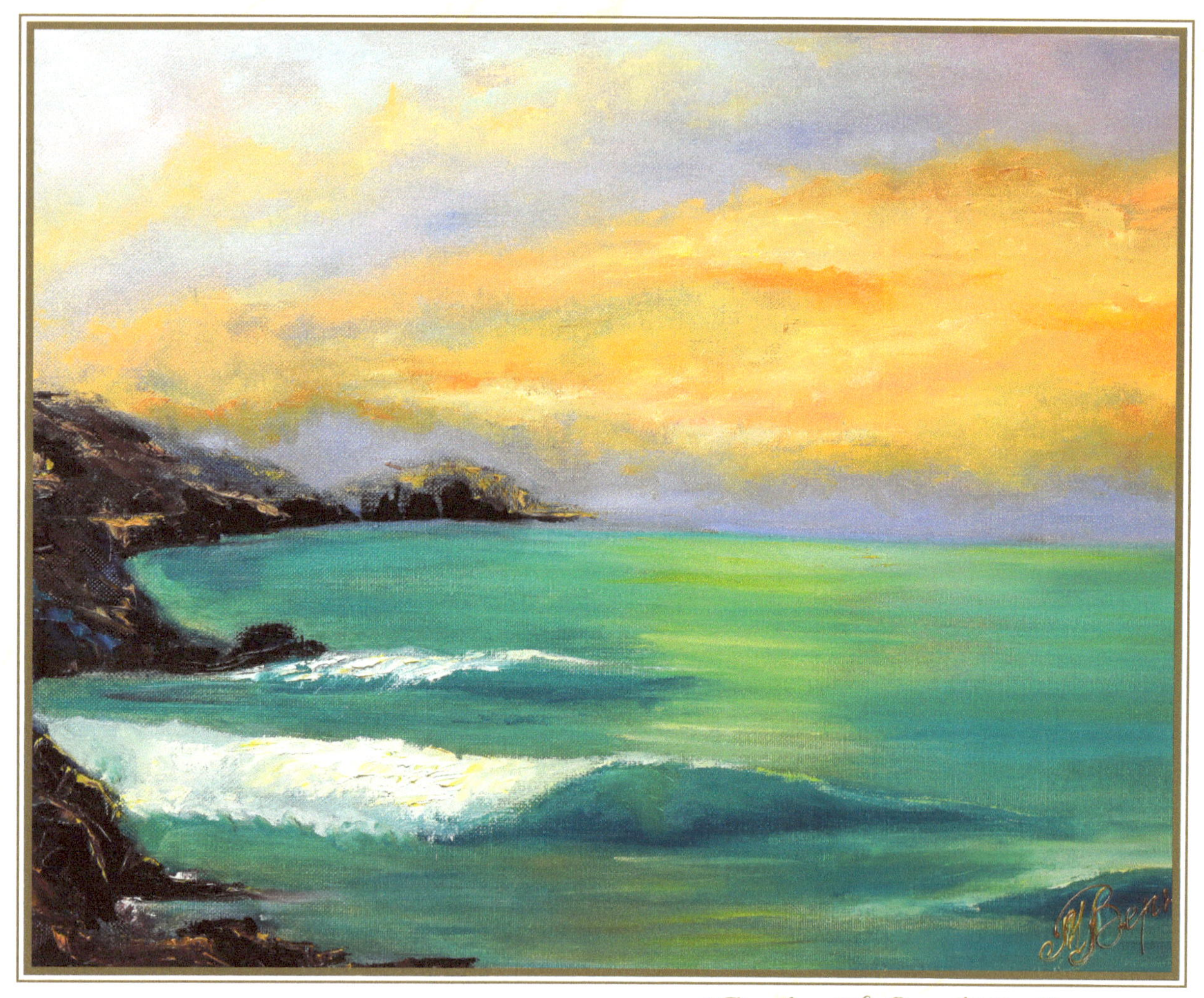

"Breathing The Sea In" Oil, Canvas, 50x70

## THE SEA AND I

The sea and I are kindred,
Like brother and sister,
Like mother and child,
Like the sky and the stars!
Out of this abyss,
As if it were yesterday
I came out salty,
And I've come out of this abyss

Walking on the waves,
Where I've walked many times,
Through the world beneath the water,
I've changed from the sea to the land!
Daughter of the sea and song,
With the colour of the sea's eyes,
Part of the surf,
I'm only listening to him!

How tender
The summer storm's furs!
My cross is not heavy,
And I'm happy everywhere!
Out of the splashes of existence,
I sew a mantilla of verse.
To decorate with it,
The shimmer of fate!

That I may shine in it
In the earth's bosom,
As I once did in the sea,
In a past life,
The waves of the earth,
As in the sea,
In my happy, terrestrial my ascent!

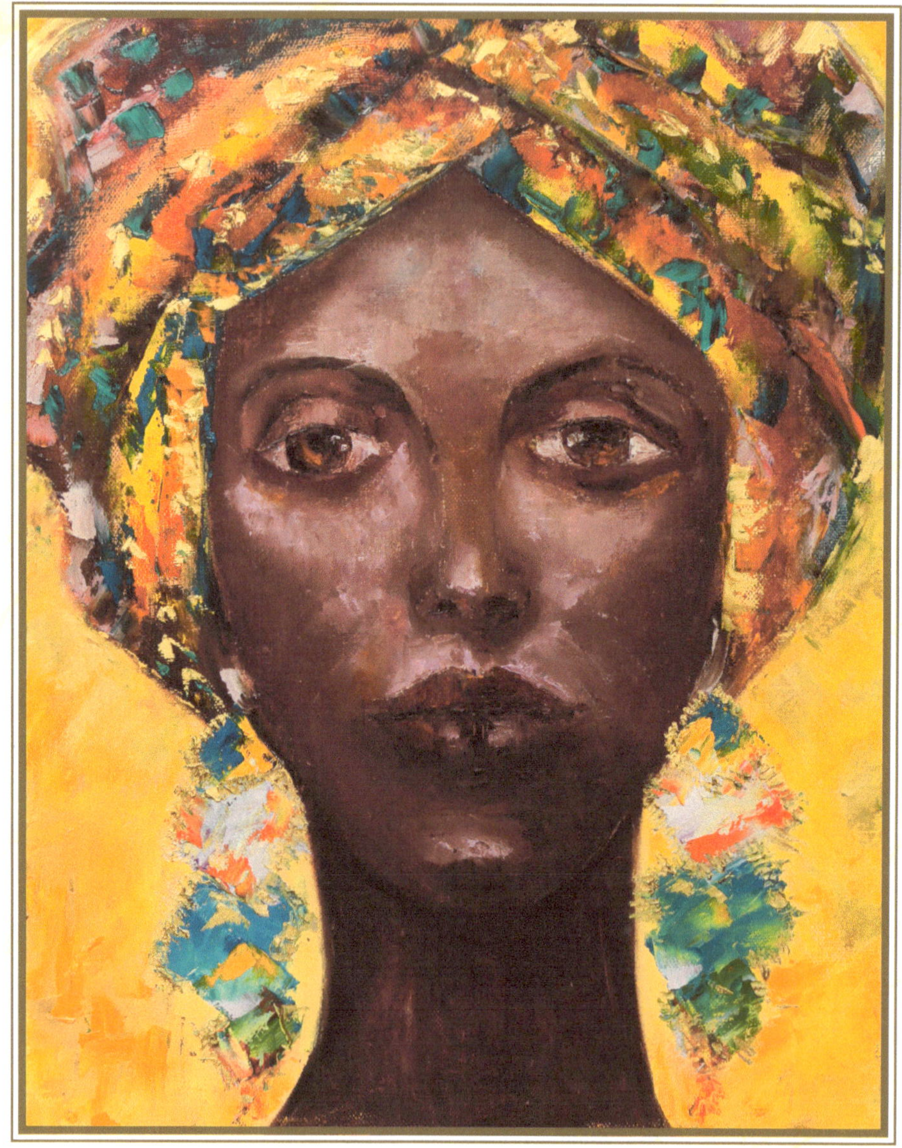

"Passion That Smells Of Cinnamon" Oil, Canvas. 60x80 (Sold)

## SACRED LOVE

Rushing down that abyss in a waterfall,
There's no point in thinking how to stay alive.
Well, is it a sin to be with you?
Well, is it a sin to love so sincerely?

We walk in embrace on a string over the abyss,
Love gives us its wings
A plea for heavenly mercy
Interprets the atonement of sin!

What is sin and what is holiness?
Only time shall make all things plain!
Mere jealousy and prejudice
Is more akin to man's sins...

Stepping into love as into an impudent abyss,
We are left to believe in one thing:
God created sin as the best reason
To show us His mercy!!!

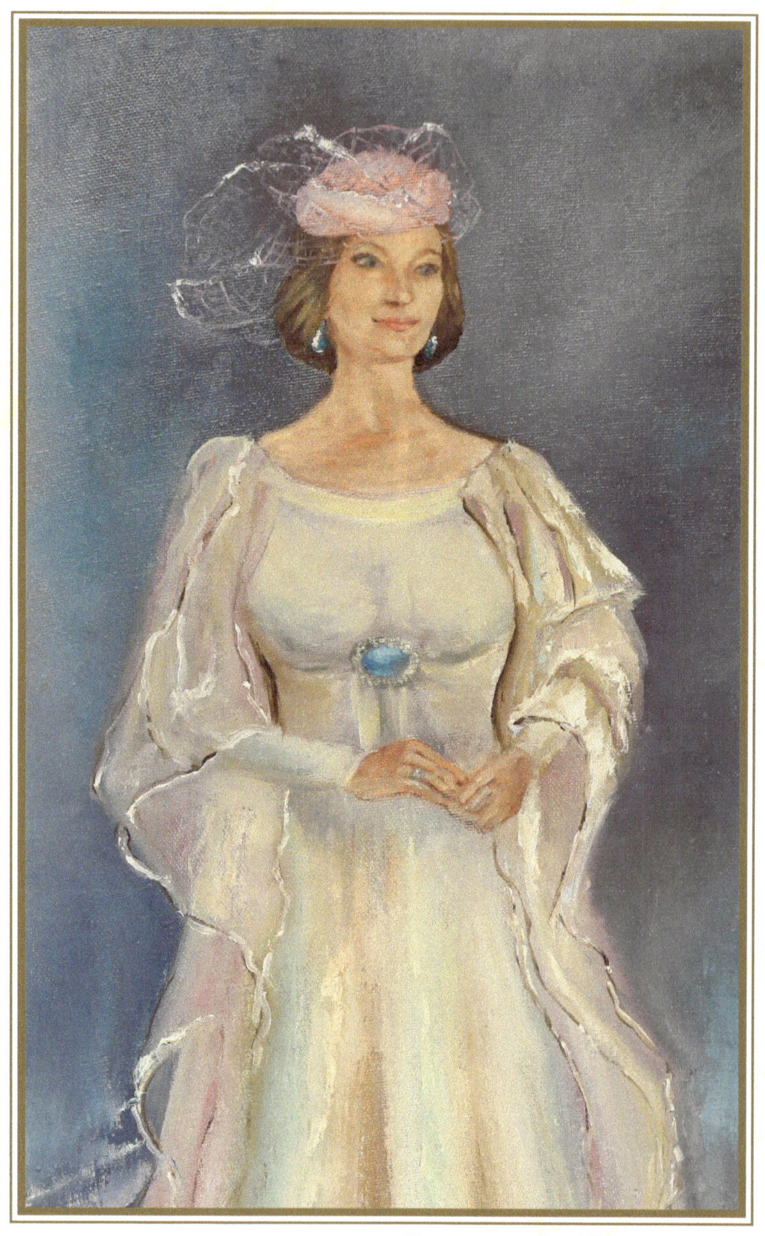

"Autoportrait" Oil, Canvas. 100x110

## SELF-PORTRAIT

I am the wind blowing, I am the anxiety,
Your unstoppable road,
I'm not to be kept on a leash.
I am a bird in the sky and in your hand!

I am this autumn, this air of blue.
I am the inspired hoarfrost on the trees
And you can't take your eyes off me
I am the one who lives laughing!

I'm the one who's been in your house lately
I'm the one who came by your fireplace, I'm the one who walks smoothly
I am the light of fire, but my fire does not burn,
I am the one that every traveller waits for...

I am that which cannot be held in the palm of your hand
And that frisky and young
The wine that now delights you,
And that too, my beloved, is me!

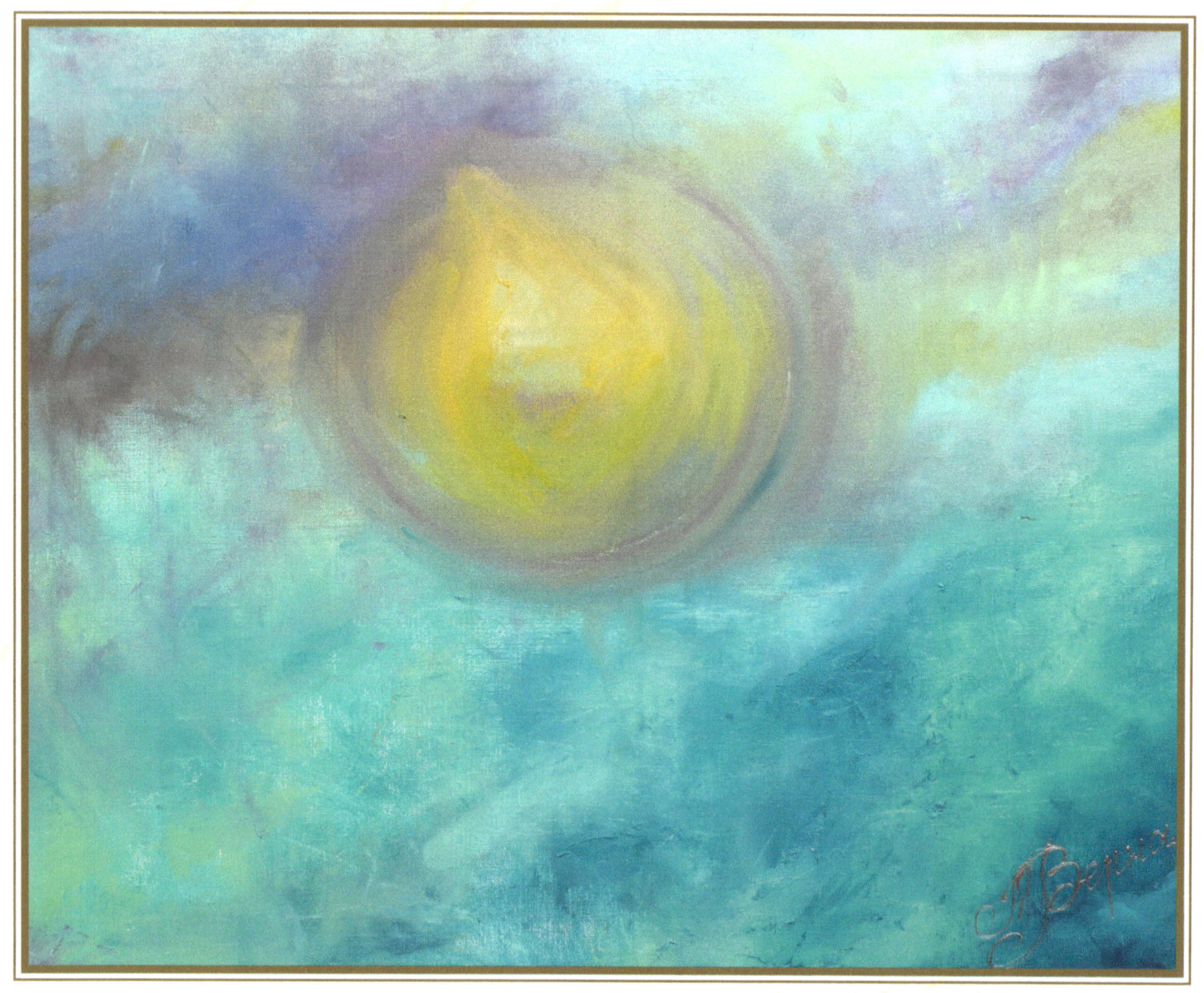

"Before Birth" Oil, Canvas. 60x80

**I AM BORN AGAIN**

I'm born again. And what's to blame?
The spring? Your words? My growing up?!
The condition falls away...
And reason finds no explanation

For change. But the mind is lonely
When the soul is silent to knowledge.
Birth and rebirth
Is appointed to us as a milestone and a confession

Of readiness to take up the new circle,
To be born again, to draw strength from the source,
From the truth that spills around,
From faith and reflection!

I am born again. And every spring
I look to the sun's rays for my handwriting.
And renewed, like leaves from the buds,
I come into the world to be myself again!

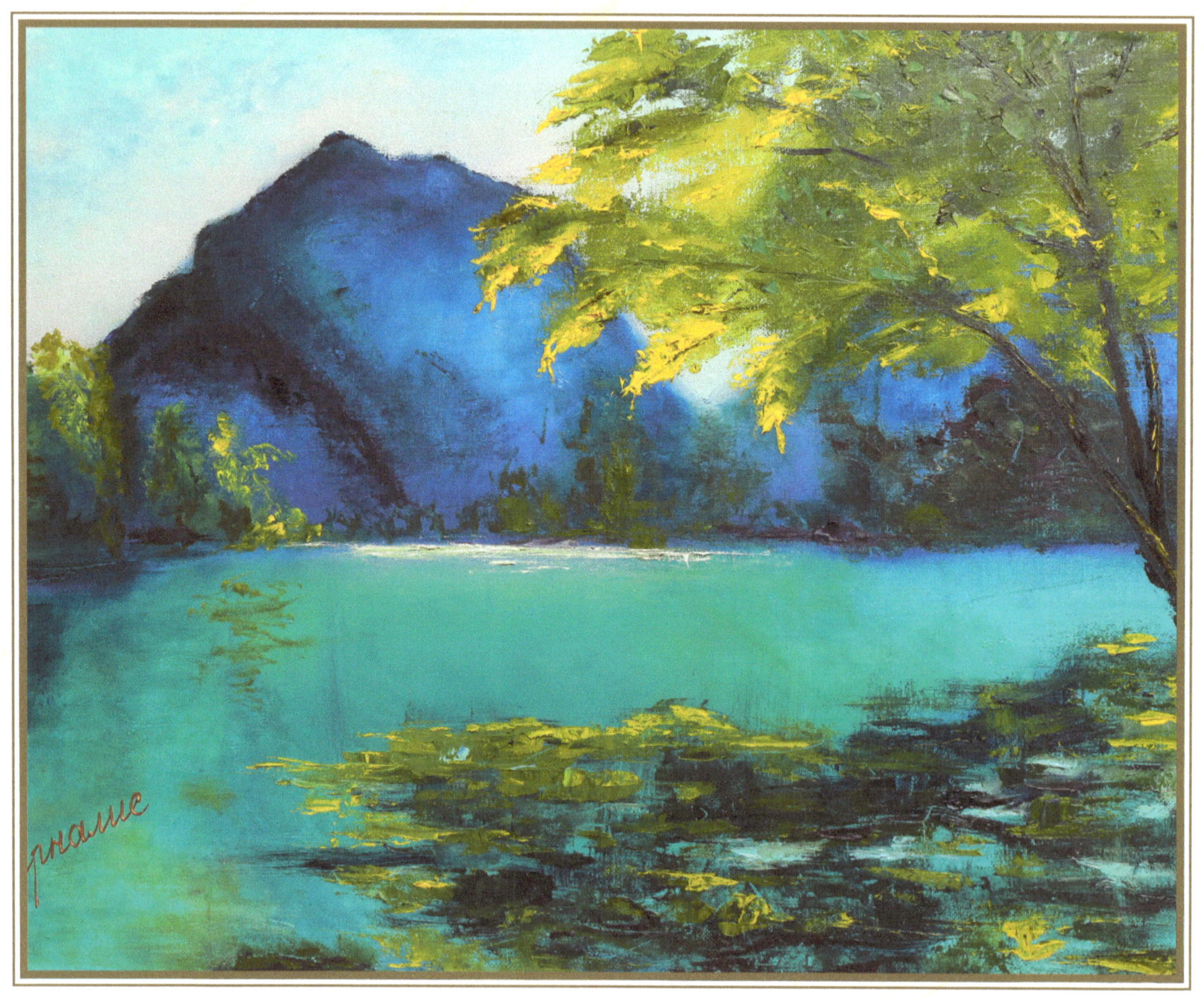

"Solitude" Oil, Canvas, 70x100

***TO LIVE IS TO REMEMBER!***

"You didn't really change. You were just becoming more and more yourself. You were going in search of the meaning of life, and as it turned out, you were going to the Real You. On your way You were losing everything extraneous, superfluous, imposed, not Yours. You were remembering Yourself..."

I realised that to live is to remember
Of myself in forgotten past incarnations.
We don't change! And do we need to change,
What is in me from God is perfect!

That's why it seems like a game
To find the mysterious meaning.
We look for meaning, just to be who we are.
And to remember, unadorned and unembarrassed

How we were conceived and transformed
In the crucible of past destinies.
Life is the mirror of the height
That brings us to ourselves... to the Present!

I have understood: to live is to remember!

# A Review of Marina Shkrobova-Vernalis' Poetry

By Shalva Amonashvili:

"I have long been fascinated by Marina Shkrobova-Vernalis' poetry. Her poems have colour, melody, sound, taste and smell - and it's all heavenly. The subtlety and wisdom of her poems is mesmerising, the images in them are like beautiful jewellery. Her poetry embraces the beauty of thought and feeling, and when she reads her poems herself, it seems to me that they become living beings and manifestations of her many faces. All Marina's poetry is filled with love for people and faith in the living heavens".

www.ingramcontent.com/pod-product-compliance
Lightning Source LLC
LaVergne TN
LVHW070219110826
845147LV00003B/608

* 9 7 8 1 9 1 3 3 5 6 7 0 5 *